# THE HIGHEST + BEST USE PLAYBOOK

Finding the Unfair Advantage Over Your Real Estate Competition

**RYAN CARR**

The Highest And Best Use Playbook:
*Finding the Unfair Advantage Over Your Real Estate Competition*

Copyright ©2022 by Ryan Carr

All rights reserved. No part of this publication may be reproduced, stored in a retrieval system, or transmitted, in any form or by any means without the prior written permission of the publisher, nor be otherwise circulated in any form of binding or cover other than that in which it is published and without a similar condition being imposed on the subsequent purchaser.

Legal Disclaimer: The contents of this book are for information purposes only. This information is not intended to replace, or supersede the advice of trained advisors who know the specifics of your situation. Always seek professional advice. I am a professional nothing.

This book is also intended to be gender neutral, inclusive, and fair to all who read it ☺

First Printing, 2022

ISBN: 978-1-7387215-0-4 (Paperback)

Published by Ryan Carr

BALMORAL
PRESS

Publisher address
Balmoral Press
6-470 King st W, Oshawa ON, L1J 2K9, Suite 245

Book Interior, Book Cover and E-book Design by Amit Dey | amitdey2528@gmail.com

# Purpose and Direction

I can't find any deals.
This market is too competitive.
The prices are too high.
Construction costs are too expensive.
I have no time.,

Does this sound like someone you know? It is perspectives like these which have been holding investors back from hidden opportunities that could change the way they perceive that next property.

Good Deals Are Found, Great Deals Are Created.

In this book, Canadian real estate entrepreneur Ryan Carr extracts the nectar from advanced real estate techniques, so you, too, can gain the unfair advantage over your real estate competition.

Within three main categories, Ryan shows you how he finds opportunity in any situation through his methods using #TheHighestAndBestUse principles of:

1. Land *(Land Planning History, Infill Development, Zoning Definitions, Severance Applications, Untapped Land, Riparian/Mineral/Subsoil/Air Rights, Land Planning Stories)*

2. Structure *(Creative Renovations, Budgeting For Profit, Structural Opportunities, Loss Avoidance, Additional Residential Units, Vanity vs. Value Markets, Teardowns vs. Reno)*

3. Your Skill Sets and Time *(Quitting Your Job, ROI ROT ROL, Delegation, Creative Financing, Eliminating Time Suckers, Business Model Comparison, Scaling for Growth, Hiring Employees)*

Throughout the Canadian specific content, Ryan defines for you what #TheHighestAndBestUse actually means through the eyes of business fundamentals.

This book is for intermediate and advanced level real estate investors who are looking to optimize their business, for real estate agents looking to provide more value to their clients, and for contractors needing a creative perspective on the construction industry.

# About the Author

Ryan Carr is a Canadian real estate entrepreneur from the Greater Toronto Area. He specializes in finding the highest and best use of real property and coaching others to do the same.

Starting his real estate journey in 2012 with a bank-sale purchase, he has since grown his net worth and rental portfolio to become a self-made multimillionaire before age thirty. Ryan is an investor, a public speaker, a coach, and a podcast host.

Follow along at
www.TheHighestAndBestUse.com

### #TheHighestAndBestUse

*Definition:*
*"The Most Profitable, Productive, or Efficient Way to Get Something Done, Somehow"*

~ Ryan Carr

**Leave a little on the table for the next guy.**

~ **Dad**

# Table of Contents

Introduction . . . . . . . . . . . . . . . . . . . . . . . . . . . . . . xv

**Chapter 1.00:** #TheHighestAndBestUse of the "Land" . . . . . . .2

    1.01 Canadian Land Ownership History . . . . . . . . . . . 3

    1.02 Land Planning History: . . . . . . . . . . . . . . . . . 5

    1.03 Historical Land Measurement . . . . . . . . . . . . . 7

    1.04 Registration Types: Land Ownership vs. Land Tenure . . . . . . . . 8

    1.05 The Ten Mile Rule and Go West Rule . . . . . . . . . . . . . 9

    1.06 Subsoil Mining and Mineral Rights . . . . . . . . . . . . . 11

    1.07 Crown Land . . . . . . . . . . . . . . . . . . . . . . . . 13

    1.08 Riparian Rights on Waterfront . . . . . . . . . . . . . . 14

    1.09 Air Rights For Sky Scrapers . . . . . . . . . . . . . . . 20

    1.10 What Is a Zoning Bylaw (ZBL) . . . . . . . . . . . . . . .25

    1.11 Land Planning Definitions: . . . . . . . . . . . . . . . .27

    1.12 Built Form and Structural Definitions (Related to Zoning Bylaw) . . 31

    1.13 Zone Definitions and Zone Symbols . . . . . . . . . . . . .34

    1.14 Examples of #TheHighestAndBestUse In Common Zones . . . . . . . 37

    1.15 Compound Zoning . . . . . . . . . . . . . . . . . . . .38

    1.16 The Housing Lifecycle . . . . . . . . . . . . . . . . . .39

    1.17 Land Planning Applications . . . . . . . . . . . . . . .40

    1.18 Land Severance Principles . . . . . . . . . . . . . . . .46

    1.19 How to Read a Legal Land Description: . . . . . . . . . . . .51

1.20  Residential Building Lot Types . . . . . . . . . . . . . . . .55

1.21  Legal Non-Conforming Uses. . . . . . . . . . . . . . . . . .60

1.22  The Local Planning Appeal Tribunal (LPAT) . . . . . . . .63

1.23  Studies, Surveys, Engineered Documentation. . . . . . . . .65

1.24  Utility Infrastructure: . . . . . . . . . . . . . . . . . . . . . .71

1.25  How to Start Designing Your Site Plan . . . . . . . . . . . .76

1.26  Real World Land Planning Stories . . . . . . . . . . . . . .80

Chapter 2.00: #TheHighestAndBestUse of the "Structure" . . . . .88

2.01  The Art of Market Comparables . . . . . . . . . . . . . . .89

2.02  Vanity vs. Value Markets . . . . . . . . . . . . . . . . . . .93

2.03  Getting Quotes/Working With Contractors: . . . . . . . . .95

2.04  Renovations That Make Money. . . . . . . . . . . . . . . .99

2.05  Renovations That Don't Make Money . . . . . . . . . . . 105

2.06  "Using the Existing Structure" for Renovations and
       Economic Feasibility Questions to Ask Yourself . . . . . . . 109

2.07  "Teardown" Structures, Values, and Process . . . . . . . . . 111

2.08  Additional Residential Dwelling Units - The Basement Apartment . 116

2.09  Additional Residential Dwelling Units - The Vertical Split . . . . . 118

2.10  Additional Residential Dwelling Units - Dwelling Units
       Within Accessory Buildings. . . . . . . . . . . . . . . . . . 119

2.11  The Yellow House Story - Where Is the Money Made? . . . . . . . 127

2.12  Alternative Construction Options For Additional Units
       and Unique Structural Renovations . . . . . . . . . . . . . 128

2.13  Unconventional Stories to Achieving Structural
       #TheHighestAndBestUse . . . . . . . . . . . . . . . . . . 136

CHAPTER 3.00: #TheHighestAndBestUse of "Your Skill Sets and Time" . . . 142

    3.01 Quitting Your Job. . . . . . . . . . . . . . . . . . . . . . . . . . . . 143

    3.02: Identifying and Changing Your Personal Growth Patterns . . . . . 145

    3.03 Setting Objectives . . . . . . . . . . . . . . . . . . . . . . . . . . . . 149

    3.04 ROI, ROT, ROL (Return on Investment/Return on Time/Return on Life) . . . . . . . . . . . . . . . . . . . . . . . . . . . . . . . . . . 151

    3.05 How to Decide When You Can't Decide . . . . . . . . . . . . . . . 153

    3.06 Identifying Project Specific Skill Sets and Requirements . . . . . . 154

    3.07 Business Style Identification Flow Chart . . . . . . . . . . . . . . . 164

    3.08 Scaling and Delegation . . . . . . . . . . . . . . . . . . . . . . . . . 167

    3.09 Profits: Fixed Costs vs. Variable Costs . . . . . . . . . . . . . . . . 171

    3.10 Markup vs. Margin: They Aren't the Same . . . . . . . . . . . . . 176

    3.11 Types of Roles in a Company: #TheHighestAndBestUse of Staff . . 178

    3.12 Treating Your Staff With Respect/Company Culture . . . . . . . . 181

    3.13 #TheHighestAndBestUse of Financing . . . . . . . . . . . . . . . . 183

    3.14 Maximizing Your Daily Efficiency . . . . . . . . . . . . . . . . . . 187

    3.15 Eliminating Time Suckers . . . . . . . . . . . . . . . . . . . . . . . 189

    3.16 Passive vs. Active Investing . . . . . . . . . . . . . . . . . . . . . . 196

    3.17 Educating Yourself . . . . . . . . . . . . . . . . . . . . . . . . . . . 198

Closing Remarks, . . . . . . . . . . . . . . . . . . . . . . . . . . . . . . . . . 208

About the Author: . . . . . . . . . . . . . . . . . . . . . . . . . . . . . . . . 209

# INTRODUCTION

**To the readers of** *#TheHighestAndBestUse Playbook*, I want to thank you for taking time out of your busy schedule to read through this and extract as much information as you can from the content.

Within three main categories, I'll show you how to find opportunity in any situation through using #TheHighestAndBestUse principles of:

1. Land
2. Structure
3. Your Own Skill Sets and Time

However you prefer to learn, this book has you covered. You can read the script like a novel or use it like a textbook. You can flip through it acutely to give you ideas for an urgent issue or digest it over time while applying the principles in your organization.

This book is written for the Canadian investor who has already done a couple of deals and is looking to continue their growth along the path of real estate, finance, construction, and business.

If you're having a hard time finding deals in an uncertain market, or struggle to find value when competing against other buyers, this is for you.

If you're a real estate service professional who is looking to add value to your existing client base, or grab that edge over the next person, this is for you.

If you're a financing expert looking to gain some insight as to what the active investor world looks like under the hood, this is for you.

If you're a contractor looking for creative ways to drive construction value to a project through strategic labour and materials use, this is for you.

If you're a business owner looking for thoughtful ways to grow your team, scale your business, and create a place where people want to work, this is for you.

As much as this book is about real estate, at its core it is a business book where bricks, sticks, dirt, and entrepreneurial tendencies bind together.

Thanks again,
**Ryan Carr**
www.TheHighestAndBestUse.com

*Chapter 1.00*

# #THEHIGHESTANDBESTUSE OF THE "LAND"

# INTRODUCTION

*"Buy land, they aren't making it anymore."*
~ Mark Twain

#TheHighestAndBestUse of land planning is the #1 economic driver in real estate fundamentals. The permitted use of a land parcel will specifically dictate a large portion of that development's end value.

In this section, we will discuss topics that range from Canadian historical land planning, general rules of thumb, and creative land use techniques, to creating value from underutilized dirt using real world examples. To keep the information consistent, I will primarily use Ontario cities and information when giving details.

These details, such as density, setbacks, municipal restrictions, commercial, retail, residential etc., all make a big impact on the direction that a developer decides to take a project.

I will show you #TheHighestAndBestUse principles in many of these sections so you can get a feel for the information being presented, and how it can be best utilized to optimize your portfolio for maximum profits.

## 1.01 Canadian Land Ownership History

*"The Crown…"*

In the 1400s, John Cabot, an Italian explorer, was the first European to locate the land of what is now known as Canada. Through several treaties, wars, and proclamations, this land was further acquired by the British and/or French monarchs in the 1600s–1700s, and transferred to the British solely through the Treaty of Paris in 1763. Following these years, several treaties and documents were signed to officially acquire and/or expropriate the indigenous peoples from their land, of which certain land rights for the indigenous peoples still exist today.

According to Wikipedia, The original document that governs much of this indigenous land activity is King George III's Royal Proclamation of 1763. The history here is extremely thick, and not the purpose of the book, but it is interesting to see how land was transitioned over the years and what leads us to where we are in modern land planning.

#TheHighestAndBestUse Quick Story:

*Prior to the Treaty of Paris, the British beat the French in a battle called the "Seven Years' War," of which the French released ownership of Canadian lands to the British…but with one exception.*

*This exception being a little island just below Newfoundland called "Saint Pierre and Miquelon." In this instance, France retained the fishing rights. To this day, there is a French colony just off Canada's eastern coast that can be visited. Bring your passport, you're going to France.*

#TheHighestAndBestUse Quick Tip:

*Given that Canadian land is technically owned by the government ("The Crown") through a "fee simple" structure, upon death of the registered landowner, the property must get transferred to that landowner's estate through a legal will. If there is no legal will, The Crown retains legal rights over the parcel as it was the original landowner to begin with. More information on "fee simple" ownership to come.*

*Cite Ref #2*

## 1.02 Land Planning History:

*"No matter where I go, I know where I came from"*

*~Jennifer Lopez*

**The beginnings of land planning stem from The Crown (British Government) of** whom deeded real property to the new settlers of Canada (British Commonwealth) in exchange for the obligation to build a residence, clear the land, farm, and maintain the roadways. This was as complex a process then, as it remains today. If the settlers requested land from The Crown (called a "settlers petition"), and this petition was granted, The Crown would release the land patent from its holdings and the applicant would be given the patent (registered ownership).

This land, called a "parcel," was typically broken up by what's called "lots and concessions" with the "concession" being the traveled roadway that a "lot" (parcel of land) fronts onto. The term "concession" is loose French translation for "row of lots," and the newly surveyed parcels were grouped together into townships for geographic reference and political purposes. The "lots and concessions" appear similar to a grid system or spreadsheet layout, see the image below for a visual reference

Using the following example, a parcel's legal description of "lots and concessions" may read like this:"*Lot 7 of Concession 4, Township Name Here*". This means the parcel of land being referred to is the seventh lot in from the edge of a township boundary, and the fourth concession is the road on which the lot fronts onto. Think of it like a mailing address, 123 Main Street, except legal descriptions were (and still are) the best way to manage the land registration process to a specified owner. Since each township is slightly different throughout the province's, a succinct knowledge of the way a legal description reads for your particular area of interest would be needed. In Ontario, a typical township measures 10 Miles (16km) across.

In Southern Ontario, almost all north/south roads eventually lead to Lake Ontario. When this occurs, townships would often label these "lots and concessions" with

letters and designations rather than a numbering system .For example, "Lot 11, Con BF A.

This would read as the eleventh lot in from the edge of a township boundary. BF stands for "broken front" because there is likely some sort of irregularity with its shape (often because of water). The letter "A" represents a lettering system that likely is preceded by B and C, and so on, which keeps the parcels in some form of systemized organization.

To simplify why this is important: On all real estate purchase agreements, there is a legal description to legally determine what property you're buying. The legal description can often lead to clues as to how the parcel came to be, and if there are any easements, right of ways, irregularities, or similar, associated with it.

*Chapter 1.00 : #TheHighestAndBestUse of the "Land"*

> **#TheHighestAndBestUse Fun Fact:**
>
> The terms "township, municipality, and county" are often interchanged in current day use depending on the geographic location. Each term has a distinct land planning political hierarchy, and the terms may be intermixed for geographic identification or political purposes. Fun fact, in a municipality the top ranking politician is called a "mayor," and in a county this position is called a "reeve."
>
> Cite Ref #1

## 1.03 Historical Land Measurement

*"1 Chain = 66' "*

**Historically, land was broken up into parcels 0.25 mile in width and 1.25 miles in length, and would total 200 acres in size.** Originally deeded in 200 acre parcels, these parcels were frequently broken up into 100acre tracts for farming or redevelopment purposes. A highly common element of modern day land planning is to find 100 acre parcels in agricultural zones, which stems from having road frontage on opposing sides of a 200 acre parcel. See image below.

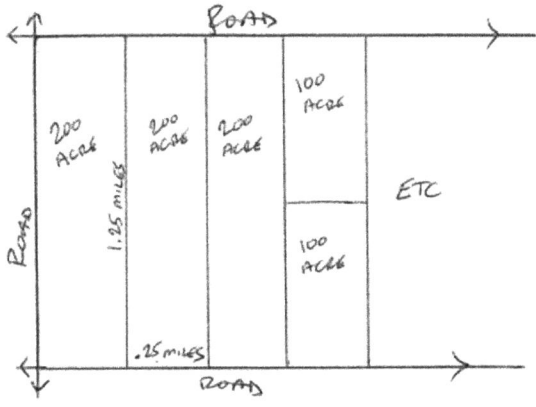

A surveyor's unit of measurement prior to modern systems was called a "chain" (remember this, it's important).

A chain contains 100 links, which equals 66 feet
1 Acre = 10 square chains
200 acres is 20x100 chains.
100 acres is 20x50 chains.

When surveyors were measuring land before the advent of electronic GPS, they would quite literally drag around metal chains from point to point. For this reason, it is quite common in older subdivisions to have lot frontages measuring 66' (1 chain) x 99' (1.5 chain) or 132' deep (2 chains).

In addition to the "chains" method, there are other ways to determine land size including "Metes and Bounds," Minutes and Hours, Degrees, Latitude/Longitude, and GPS.

## 1.04 Registration Types: Land Ownership vs. Land Tenure

*"…which you pay property tax to a form of government, and failure to do so would result in repossession."*

<u>Types of Ownership</u>

**There are two types of land ownership, "land tenure" and "absolute ownership."**

*Land Tenure*
"Land tenure" is effectively the right to the land for exclusive use, of which others cannot trespass or disturb. Also known as "the right to occupy, possess, use, or enjoy the land," this is commonly known in Canadian law as "fee simple" ownership, and comes with restrictions from a higher level of government (The Crown). The land title holder may be the registered owner of the land, but the lands are still subject to a superior landlord's (governmental)taxes, levies, and planning regulations for

use in continued fashion. An example of this may be your primary residence, of which you pay property tax to a form of government, and failure to do so would result in repossession.

*Absolute Ownership*

"Absolute ownership," also known as "allodial ownership" is the rights to the subject land exclusively, disallowing the ability of repossession, and/or possessing the requirement for taxes and levies to be paid to a higher political power. The term allodial means "land exempt from feudal duties (fax)," and "ownership by occupancy and/or by defense."

This type of ownership is rare but sometimes exists in some US states. An oversimplified example of this would be automobile ownership. In this situation, there is a legal registration process to which the vehicle is registered to an owner directly, however, there are no fees to be paid to uphold this ownership and it may never be repossessed for nonpayment of annual dues.

## 1.05 THE TEN MILE RULE AND GO WEST RULE

*"Historically, wealthy money didn't want to smell the factories they owned, so they lived upwind."*

**When we look at aerial maps between existing cities and small towns, it becomes** quite apparent that from town to town a similarity in separating distances exists. Prior to the internal combustion engine, horse and buggy, or foot travel were the chosen methods of transportation. In order to increase efficiency and provide service to local settlers, small towns on average consisted of a general store (amongst other things) and were typically placed ten miles from one another. If we draw an equidistant radius around each town center, the radii would intersect at the five mile point, which means that no person would have to travel any further than five miles to pickup supplies or deliver goods.

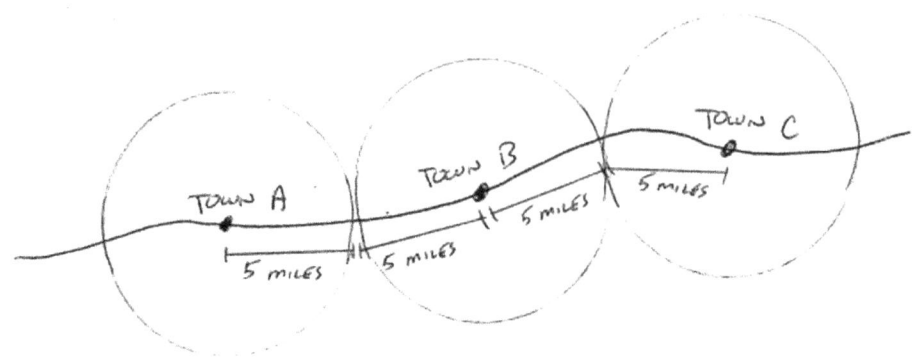

A similar land planning ideology that remains in existence today is due to the advent of the smoke stack. Using the City of Toronto, Ontario as the epicenter for comparison, moving west is a trend of increasingly expensive real estate, and moving east is a trend of lower average values. This has to do partly with being further away from "the big city," but also heavily relies on weather patterns to carry smoke away from dwellings and into areas of lesser impact. Historically, wealthy money didn't want to smell the factories they owned, so they lived upwind.

Today, land is increasingly more valuable as residential because employment lands are less economically efficient when compared to the cost benefits of offshore manufacturing.

Cite Ref #1

## 1.06 Subsoil Mining and Mineral Rights

*"Staking Your Claim"*

**In Canada, The Crown Patent (original land title) may outline whether or not the** parcel of land has the following land-use permissions: Subsoil mining and mineral rights (underground resources), above grade surface rights (the right to build on or use the land), riparian rights (as discussed in the next chapter), or other rights pertaining to the surveyed boundary.

In Ontario, multiple rights to the land may be held simultaneously by more than one party. For example, a titled landowner may hold the "surface rights" to travel upon the land, while another party may hold the mineral and mining rights to extract resources beneath it. A logging company may also hold the rights to the trees, while at the same time, a lease holder may lease rights to the soil, sand, and gravel explicitly.

While this is a highly complicated topic, most land in Canada retains surface rights by default but does not include subsurface rights. If you've ever installed a water well at a rural property, a permit is required. That permit is a governmental levy that's paid by the landowner to extract water for residential uses.

#TheHighestAndBestUse Story

*The provincial government typically regulates <u>subsurface</u> (underground) rights for mining natural resources with short/long-term leases in exchange for payment. This allows a company to mine for those resources, but it doesn't mean they can park their equipment above the mine.*

*If a private landowner owns the property above the mine, this generally means the private landowner also retains ownership of the <u>surface</u> rights. The mining company then has two options: rent the surface from the landowner to park mining equipment directly above the mine or get creative.*

> *In true #TheHighestAndBestUse form, a mining company may opt to purchase an adjacent parcel of land for directional bore drilling, tunnel boring, fracking, and blasting underneath the surface of the land they couldn't rent to begin with.*
>
> *In rare cases, historic land patents have granted the landowner the subsurface rights in full without a lease.*
>
> Cite #3

### *"Staking a Claim"*

In order to mine subsoil minerals, mining companies must "stake a claim" (tell the government they found something worth mining) on the area, and then apply to mine the area through political procedures. The minimum size of land you may stake is sixteen hectares, while the maximum size is 256 hectares. This prevents companies from over staking and hoarding land, and ensures there is enough room on the site to make a claim profitable should mineral deposits be found. A mining company cannot stake a claim on land where a residential dwelling, church, cemetery, public building, artificial reservoir, spring, outhouse, orchard, or farm (where crops may be damaged) exists.

If you have heard the term "stake your claim," it comes from the mining industry. Staking a claim stems back to locating a potential mine and marking the perimeter of the area with blaze paint or flags. This idiom has carried through to present day verbiage in many forms, and loosely defines someone marking their territory over an item or location.

Again, through a highly detailed historical search at a land registry office (LRO), the original Crown Patent will detail the specificities to the parcel of land on a microfiche record…

Readers: visit this website for highly detailed info on mining rights and subsurface rights.https://www.canaryinstitute.ca/publications/Understanding_Mining_Rts.pdf

## 1.07 CROWN LAND

*"Crown land is kept in holdings for  
The Crown to lease out for monetary gain."*

**Crown land is considered land that has been retained by The Crown (government,** provincial, and federal) and has not been given, sold, designated, or delegated to any private person, family, trust, or corporation.

Ontario Crown Land makes up approximately 89% of Ontario, 92% of Quebec, and 95% of Newfoundland/Labrador. Overall, less than 11% of the land within Canada's borders are held by private citizens.

When viewed in this manner it places perspective on political policy as to why people reside in major cities vs. urban sprawl. Environmental concerns, political views, carbon tax, municipal servicing, roadway maintenance, emergency services, etc, all come into play here.

Crown land is kept in holdings for The Crown to lease out for monetary gain in the form of logging, mining, energy, water resources, or other industrial purposes. The funds collected from commercial leasing are funneled back into the economy to formulate part of provincial and federal government annual revenue targets. Crown land can be purchased by way of bid or tender through a formal application, provided it has been declared as surplus. There are many restrictions on acquiring this type of land.

> **#TheHighestAndBestUse Quick Tip**
>
> **Public uses for Crown land without need direct ownership/active lease are as follows:**
>
> *Camping up to twenty-one days*
>
> *Hiking*
>
> *Waterskiing*
>
> *ATV and snowmobiling (provided motorized vehicles are not restricted)*
>
> *Fishing (provided you hold a valid provincial fishing license)*
>
> *Canoeing*
>
> *Bird-watching*
>
> *Hunting (provided you hold a valid hunting license/no restrictions)*
>
> *Horseback riding*
>
> *Cite #4*

## 1.08 Riparian Rights on Waterfront

*"Ripa," meaning bank or shore.*

**If you are a land developer, cottage owner, waterfront lover, or environmentalist,** this chapter will resonate with you. Riparian rights are a landowners right for the use of a watercourse adjacent to, or within, their property's boundaries. The term "riparian" is used to describe the water where land meets liquid. Similar terms such as "riparian vegetation" (riverside plant growth) or "riparian wildlife" (animals near/in the water) relate to items surrounding the watercourse.

"Riparian" comes from the Latin term "Ripa" meaning bank or shore. Some examples of riparian rights may be public access to the water, swimming, fishing, anchoring a boat, underwater mining, log floating, residential consumption, farming, irrigation, he right of access, the right of water quality, the right of natural flow, and the right for personal use.

Waterfront landowners will notice that, oftentimes on a land survey, the riparian rights will be documented showing the property boundary "to the water's edge." If a landowner owns waterfront up to the "water's edge," that land is set to fluctuate based on tidal tendencies or erosion. Private ownership in this form prevents the general public from docking of boats or accessing the soil beyond this point.

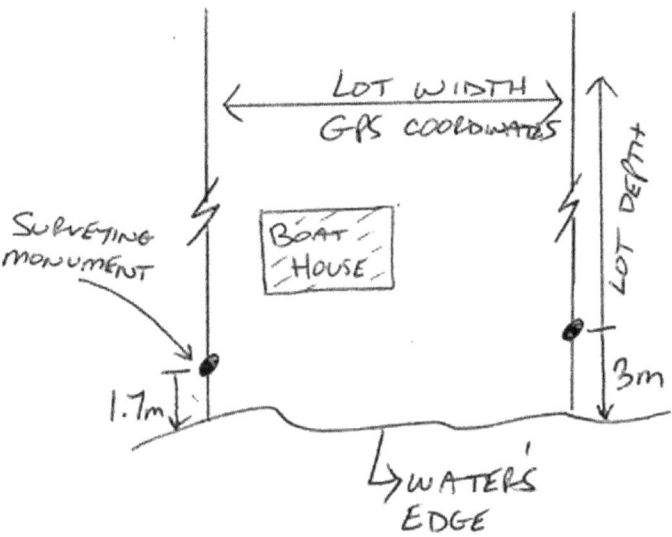

Something to consider: If land is naturally eroded, it will become part of The Crown (government) holdings and would require permission to reclaim back as privately held property. The opposite of this is called "land accretion," defined as the gradual addition of matter (to accumulate). In the case of land planning for riparian purposes, this would be defined as the natural addition of soils to the water's edge over time.

This is common in areas such as waterfront property where the shoreline continues to be eroded overtime by waves or beach sand piles up to create dunes. This land can be added, or taken away, to a landowners holdings.

> **# TheHighestAndBestUse Real World Example**
>
> *If a landowner holds legal title to a peninsula of land, and a natural disaster washes away a portion of that land into a watercourse, the landowner may no longer own the soil that once formed part of their property boundary. If this washout occurred at an access point (like a driveway), a backfill permit/causeway/bridge permit would now be required because the watercourse is owned by the government.*
>
> *#TheHighestAndBestUse here would be to do one of two things: Put it back exactly the way it was or use this opportunity to enhance long-term stability and also make it unique. A driveway is nice but a bridge is a selling feature. One of my coaching students bought a property where access to the home required crossing a river. After deliberating several options, a bridge was installed. How many houses can say they have a moat?*
>
> *Cite 5*

### *Navigable vs. Non-Navigable Waterways:*

The term navigable vs. non-navigable waterway when determining riparian rights or ownership of a waterway is highly subjective and can only be decided by existing land record or a presiding court. As a general rule, a navigable waterway is determined by the ability for public use from one public point of access to another. For example, can someone drop in a kayak and move fluidly from A to B?

Non-navigable waterways would be the exact opposite—the waterway is low flow and shallow rendering it useless for these purposes. Various details for determining this include depth, flow, length of navigability, public or private access points, previous land patents or riparian rights granted to date, historical records of depth/direction/flow, chain of ownership, seasonality, etc.

**Case Study Below:**

As Per Government of Ontario Case Law

*"In essence, the test of navigability developed in Canada is one of public utility. If a waterway has real or potential practical value to the public as a means of travel or transport from one point of public access to another point of public access, the waterway is considered navigable…navigability should depend on public utility. If the waterway serves, or is capable of serving, a legitimate public interest in that it is, or can be, regularly and profitably used by the public for some socially beneficial activity, then assuming the waterway runs from one point of public access to another point of public access, it must be regarded as navigable land as within the public domain."*

*Justice Doherty accepted the following seven conclusions reached previously in the Coleman case:*

1. *Navigability in law requires that the waterway be navigable in fact. It must be capable in its natural state of being traversed by large or small craft of some sort;*

2. *Navigable also means floatable in the sense that the river or stream is used or is capable of use for floating logs or log rafts or booms;*

3. *A river may be navigable over part of its course and not navigable over other parts;*

4. *To be navigable, a river need not, in fact, be used for navigation so long as it is realistically capable of being so used;*

5. *A river is not necessarily navigable if it is used only for private purposes or if it is used for purposes which do not require transportation along the river (i.e., fishing);*

6. *Navigation need not be continuous, but may fluctuate with the seasons; and*

7. *Where a proprietary interest asserted depends on a Crown grant, navigability is initially to be determined as at the date of The Crown grants (in this case, 1821 and 1822).*

*Based on the Canoe Ontario ruling, the Ministry of Natural Resources, in addition to considering the above noted seven conclusions, will be guided by the following key points when making navigability decisions for administrative purposes:*

1. *For purposes of determining navigability, the Ministry position will only be finalized after considering the issue of navigability from the perspective of both the date of inspection and the date of letters patent. The necessity to consider navigability from both perspectives arises because the courts have historically considered navigability at the date of the grant, but it is possible, but not certain that future decisions will reflect only the current situation.*

2. *Navigability depends on public utility.*

3. *Public utility means actual or potential commercial or recreational use, or other socially beneficial activity.*

4. *Generally, the waterway should run from one point of public access to another point of public access.*

5. *Seasonal limitations do not detract from navigability as long as there is some use (or potential use) which is regular and which has practical value.*

**New Waterfront Developments Don't Automatically Get Riparian Rights**

In many newer developments or land severances on waterfront, riparian rights are NOT included within the parcel boundaries. It's common practice for a governing agency to expropriate the first number of feet from the high watermark and maintain exclusive ownership to the water's edge.

For example, when a parcel of land is rezoned or severed on a major arterial road, a municipality may expropriate a section of land, often considered a "road widening allowance." This land is conveyed to the government for future use as a condition of severance approval. The same thing may happen with the water's edge.

Unknowingly to the applicant, this land may actually form part of the public domain, and although it would be highly unusual for someone else to dock their boat on what "feels like" your waterfront lot, they may actually be within their rights to do so provided they don't come onto your private land boundary. Waterfront homeowners, this means you.

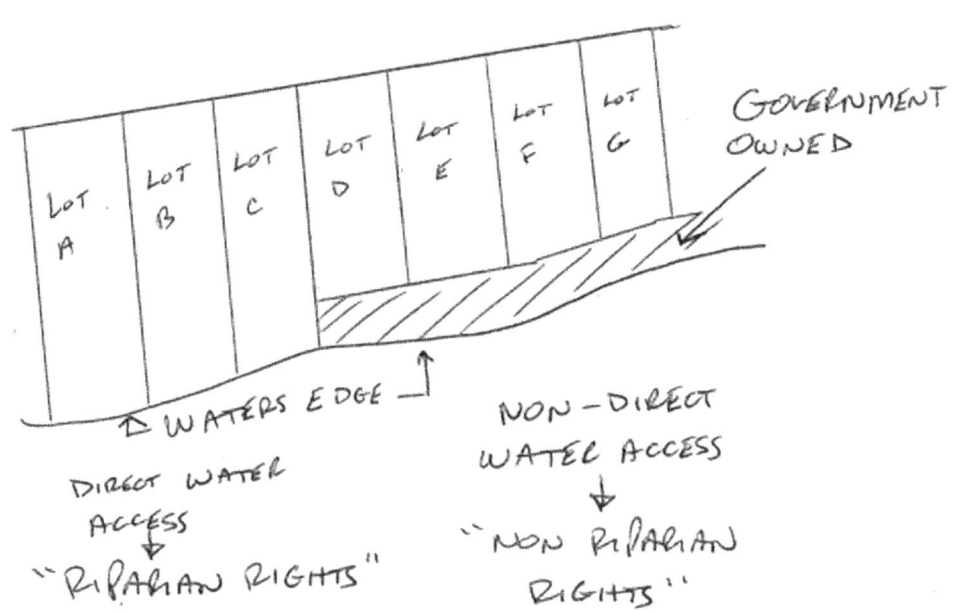

**Agricultural Riparian Uses**

Riparian rights also regulate the use of the watercourse for items such as irrigation. The riparian documents pertaining to this would generally permit the use of such water determined by the frontage along the river's edge, based on volumetric consumption, and prohibit the overuse of said water if it affects an adjoining riparian right holder. In simple terms, you can only use so much water, and you can't affect the next person downstream by starving them out.

> **#TheHighestAndBestUse Quick Story**
>
> *In the Netflix TV Show Ozark, one of the lead characters owned a poppy farm near a public watercourse. This watercourse sat relatively docile until the landowner realized that damming up of the adjacent farmland would connect their small river to a navigable waterway owned by the United States government. By doing so, their non-navigable watercourse would become navigable.*
>
> *Within this jurisdiction, navigable waterways permit the use of riverboat casinos. Although their previously owned land would have been partially turned over to the government for riparian uses, the overall value of the parcel would exponentially increase. How's that for #TheHighestAndBestUse?*

## 1.09 Air Rights For Sky Scrapers

> *"One of the most high profile Air Rights cases was over the historic landmark of Grand Central Terminal."*

*Air Rights*
**Traditionally in larger cities like Toronto, Ontario, or New York City, New York,** Air Rights above a parcel of land are a very big deal. In a similar fashion to owning subsoil rights below grade in pursuit of mining exploration, "Air Rights" are the regulation mechanism to control maximum building height in urban settings. Large scale buildings are constructed using many zoning techniques to sculpt their design, two of which include "Air Rights" and "Floor Area Ratio" (FAR).

Using a four-building city block for example, and assuming each of the buildings can be built utilizing "Air Rights" to dictate height and built form, let's approach this in the most simple way.

- All buildings may be 100m in height as per zoning
- Building A is proposing 100m

- Building B is Proposing 100m
- Building C is proposing 80m
- Building D is proposing 120m

Building A and B are within the regulations of their "Air Rights" which means they are good to proceed. Building C and D, however, have negotiated the Air Rights in a buy-and-sell type fashion. While building C is proposing 80m in height, they have agreed to sell the additional 20m to building D, likely for a fee. From a planning and economic perspective, there may be several reasons for this.

Potential Reasons For Building C to Sell Air Rights:

- Perhaps, the subsoil conditions won't permit an additional 20m of height.
- Perhaps, the wind currents in that direction are unfavourable for engineering.
- Perhaps, the financing is restricted to a maximum allowable dollar amount.
- Recoup construction cost.
- Financial or environmental constraints.

Rather than letting the Air Rights go to waste, developers convey those rights to another building because the sum total of the city block still falls within compliance. Sometimes, lot mergers will occur in order to combine the Air Rights of multiple parcels of land together, and sometimes <u>existing</u> buildings may sell their Air Rights outright, knowing that the future of their existing building will never be altered (historical buildings).

*Floor Area Ratio*
"Floor Area Ratio" (FAR) is defined as the "numerical value of the building's floor area relative to the site upon which it is located." This calculation is used to determine the height of a building vs. the combined square footage of each level within that building.

For example, if you have a land parcel of 20m x 20m (400 square meters) and a Floor Area Ratio of 2:1, your building would be permitted to have 800 square meters of floor space. This may work out to a two-storey building at 400sm per floor, a four-storey building at 200sm per floor, or some other combination there in.

As a rule, the higher in elevation you go, the better the view and the more each unit is worth. An important inverse to unit value is construction cost. The higher up you go, the more engineering is required and the trickier it is to build. Over the years, as zoning and regulations change, massive amounts of value can become unlocked simply from policies allowing additional FAR.

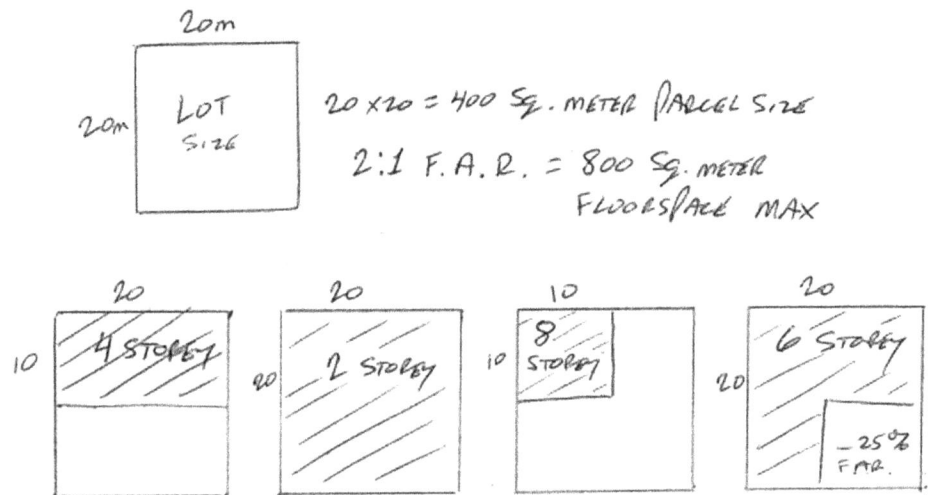

### *Additional Information*

Air Rights can also be transferred in the form of an easement, preventing future buildings from blocking natural daylight into adjacent building windows. Take for example a multitude of buildings overlooking Central Park in Manhattan. Can you imagine the outrage if a new developer comes along and pops a mega-building in front of your $100million penthouse condo? This is a very real circumstance that sales professionals selling property, where the view is a driving factor in purchase price, should be aware of.

In smaller cities and periphery towns, building height is controlled through preset height limitations in the zoning bylaw (e.g., your house can only be X meters tall) and FAR doesn't apply.

> ### Grand Central Terminal's Air Rights - Story
>
> *One of the most high profile Air Rights cases was over the historic landmark of Grand Central Terminal in Manhattan, New York. As written in the New York Times, March 2018 (Charles V. Bagli).*
>
> *"The owners of Grand Central Terminal are selling Air Rights for about $240 million to JP Morgan Chase so the bank can build its new Midtown Manhattan headquarters, according to executives who have been briefed on the deal.... Six months after the city rezoned the area surrounding Grand Central Terminal to allow for ever taller skyscrapers and the transfer of Air Rights from existing buildings, huge real estate deals are underway across the 78-block district called Midtown East."*
>
> *The verbiage continued on to discuss the tremendous benefits of "up-zoning" specific areas of the city that required the most change and had the most potential.*
>
> *Overall, this was a massive deal that allowed new lifeblood to be pumped into Manhattan while utilizing "found value" strategies above a building that would never be taken down. Grand Central Terminal is one of the most iconic buildings in New York City, and the article further went on to discuss how the City of New York would receive a portion of the sale proceeds, plus 5% of the sale proceeds would be reserved to maintain and preserve the historic building. This is #TheHighestAndBestUse of land planning and structure planning.*

**Toronto CN Railyards Air Rights - Story**

*Downtown Toronto (Ontario) is a metropolitan hotspot—Toronto Maple Leafs, Toronto Raptors, Toronto Blue Jays, Toronto Rock. A city with all the major sports teams, tons of history, and a financial center of global magnitude. The City of Toronto, headed by Mayor John Tory, is proposing to acquire the Air Rights to a parcel of land located above CN Rail's railway tracks. The proposal is to acquire the land and convert this dead airspace into a park for city residents to enjoy year round.*

*As noted on a Toronto.com article written by Tess Kalinowski in January 2020,*

*"Rail Deck Park" is the name of the project, Tory (City Mayor) said. The city's efforts to acquire the land from another developer have been ongoing for a number of years. "At the end of it you're going to own some of the real estate/Air Rights necessary to proceed with the first phase of the park," he said. "If you don't have the real estate it doesn't mean much."*

*Discussion of the Rail Deck Park always envisioned it as a phased project, said Coun. Joe Cressy (Ward 10, Spadina-Fort York). Because of the negotiations over Air Rights, city officials have been reluctant to assign a timeline to the first phase of the park...*

*It later went on to discuss in the article that nobody was willing to speculate on the value of the Air Rights above these train tracks, but an acre of land for development typically sells in the $70 –100 million range. As this is planned for park land, and not for development, the land values would be significantly less.*

*Cite 6*

## 1.10 What Is a Zoning Bylaw (ZBL)

*"To summarize, the ZBL dictates what you can build, and where you can build it."*

A ZONING BYLAW (ZBL) IS A WRITTEN GOVERNMENT DOCUMENT THAT DICTATES specifically what a parcel of land may be utilized for in any given town, state, province, county, municipality, or jurisdiction. A zoning bylaw is often hundreds of pages in length and outlines every specific land use category (zone), with very specific terminology that pertains to that land use. Once you pick a geographic region that you're looking to develop land in, learning the zoning bylaw will become second nature and a mandatory practice because this is where your land value will be derived from.

From site to site, or city to city, every zoning bylaw will vary. Even if you're looking at doing a project just a few lots away from an existing project, or in a city nearby, the rules and regulations may change. The definitions within that zoning bylaw are stated below, followed by an example of what a zoning bylaw actually looks like.

For many examples in this book, I will be using the City of Oshawa zoning bylaw 60-94, as found at www.oshawa.ca. To the best of my understanding, this is public information from a government resource.

To summarize, the ZBL dictates what you can build, and where you can build it.

> #### #TheHighestAndBestUse Quick Story About Property Tax:
>
> *In the 1600s, King Louis XIV of the French monarch placed "restrictive covenants" on the (now Canadian) lands which had to be abided by as a citizen land holder under French rule. These covenants (also known as property tax) were paid in one of three ways: labour, currency, or agricultural production.*

*As time passed and in order to subsidize income potential, landowners began subdividing their parcels in ways that were less productive for agriculture and reduced the income that could be generated. Since the French king always needed to be paid, in 1744, restrictions were placed on the way in which the land could be divided up to maximize the efficiency of the crop production and maintain road frontage for ease of transporting goods.*

*Since land parcels were traditionally longer in dimension then they were wide, and road frontage was typically on the narrow facing edge, every time a parcel of land was subdivided it became further narrowed to the point that it was no longer economically feasible to sustain agricultural use.*

*In its most primitive form, the "zoning bylaw" was born, and in 1795, the Ontario land registry system was conceived. To this day, through microfiche records and the Ontario land registry office, you are able to view the original land patents and see the chain of ownership history for many parcels.*

*Cite 6.5*

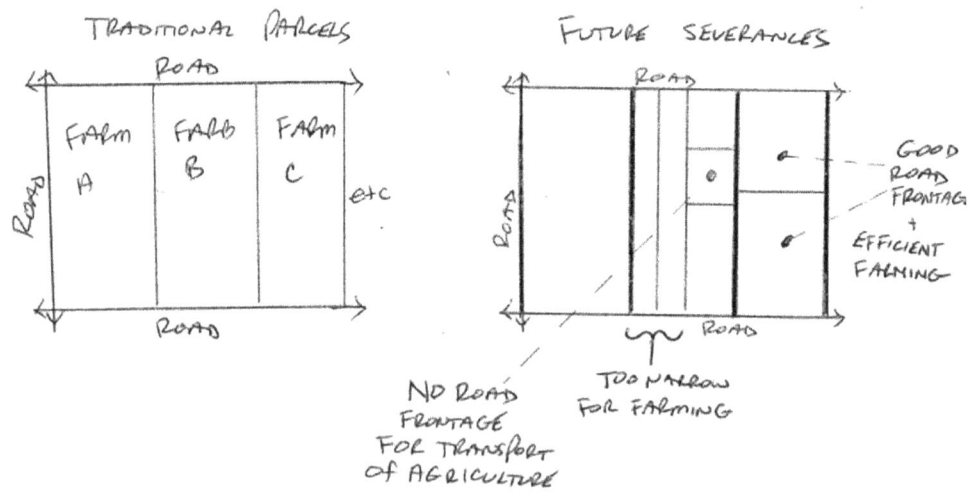

## 1.11 Land Planning Definitions:

*""SETBACK" means the shortest distance between  
a property line…"*

Each ZBL has a section within it called "definitions." The definitions are what define the use and meaning of a word that governs the use of land, or the structures that sit upon it.

These definitions will be used throughout the book. If needed, flip back to this section from time to time to make sure you're understanding them correctly.

### <u>Land Planning Definitions</u> (Oshawa ZBL 60-94)

"LOT" means a parcel of land which is:

a. Shown as a lot or block on a registered plan of subdivision; or

b. Described in a single transfer/deed of land of legal effect registered in the Land Registry Office or the Land Titles Office for the Land Registry Division of Durham.

"LOT AREA" means the total horizontal area within the lot lines of a lot.

"LOT COVERAGE" means that percentage of the lot area covered by all buildings above ground level, excluding building features that project beyond the main walls of a building such as window sills, cornices, pilasters, cantilevered canopies or roofs, eaves, gutters, bay windows, chimney breasts, unenclosed decks, unenclosed porches or unenclosed platforms, and cantilevered balconies whether open or enclosed. (39-2004).

"LOT DEPTH" means the horizontal distance between the front and rear lot lines but, where the front and rear lot lines are not parallel, the lot depth is the length of a line joining the midpoints of such lot lines.

"LOT FRONTAGE" means the length of that segment of a straight line contained within a lot which is parallel to a line which joins the points of intersection of the side lot lines with the front lot line and which is a perpendicular distance of 6m from the front lot line (66-1998).

"LOT LINE" means any boundary of a lot.

"STOREY" means a part of a building which is not a half-storey and which is situated between any floor level and the floor, ceiling or roof above it, but shall not include a basement, cellar, or attic.

"SIGHT TRIANGLE" means a triangular space bounded by the two straight lines which contain the defining angle of a corner lot and a straight line connecting the two points on the aforementioned two straight lines which are at a distance of 6m from the point of their intersection.

"SIDE LOT LINE" means a lot line other than a front lot line or rear lot line.

"SIDE YARD" means a yard extending from the front yard to the rear yard between the side lot line and the wall of any building or structure on the lot.

"YARD" means any portion of a lot which is unoccupied by buildings or structures, except as accessory uses expressly permitted in this bylaw.

"YARD DEPTH" means the shortest distance between the lot line forming one limit of the yard and any point in the wall of the building or structure forming the other limit of the yard in question.

"SETBACK" means the shortest distance between a property line of a lot and the nearest part of any building, structure, excavation, or outdoor storage on a lot (66–1998).

"REAR LOT LINE" means the lot line which is opposite the front lot line provided, however, that where the lot line opposite the front lot line is not a straight line, a straight line 6m in length, which is entirely within the lot and at the maximum possible distance from and parallel to a line joining the points of intersection of the side lot lines with the front lot line, shall be deemed to be the rear lot line.

"PARKING SPACE" means an unobstructed and maintained surfaced area, exclusive of driveways, aisles, ramps, or columns, provided for the purpose of storing or parking one vehicle for purposes other than for the display or offering for sale of such vehicle.

"LANDSCAPED OPEN SPACE" means open space on a lot which is used for landscaping of any kind or land which is used for any accessory recreational purpose and notwithstanding the generality of the foregoing, includes lawns, flower beds, shrubbery, trees and other plantings, decorative pools, ponds and other natural water bodies, private walkways, patios, unenclosed porches, tennis courts, shuffleboard courts, playgrounds, swimming pools, pool areas, decks, and similar recreational facilities but does not include any parking space, aisle, driveway, or loading space.

"HEIGHT" means, when used in reference to a building or structure, the vertical dimension between the grade of such building or structure and:

   a. In the case of a flat roof, the highest point of the roof surface or parapet wall;

   b. In the case of a mansard roof, the deck line;

   c. In the case of a gable, hip, gambrel, or one-slope roof, the average level between eaves and ridge, except that a one-slope roof having a slope of less than twenty (20) degrees from the horizontal shall be considered a flat roof for the purposes of this bylaw;

   d. In the case of a structure not having a roof, the top of such structure; or

   e. Where an exterior wall other than a required fire wall extends above the top of the roof of a building, the top most part of such exterior wall.

"FRONT LOT LINE" means the lot line that abuts an improved street.

"FRONT YARD" means a yard extending across the full width of a lot between the front lot line and the nearest wall of any main building or structure on the lot.

"DENSITY" means the ratio between the number of dwelling units located or proposed to be located on a lot and the lot area, expressed in units per hectare. In the application of this definition, the number of dwelling units permitted shall be rounded to the nearest whole number.

"DEVELOPMENT" means the erection or placing of one or more buildings or structures on land or the making of an addition or alteration to a building or structure that has the effect of substantially increasing the size or usability thereof, or the laying out or establishment of a commercial parking lot.

"CORNER LOT" means a lot, the street line, or street lines of which is/are composed of two or more straight lines, or of one or more curves, or of any combination of a straight line or straight lines and a curve or curves, such that the defining angle is not greater than one hundred and thirty-five (135) degrees.

"BASEMENT" means that part of a building which is between two floor levels and is partly below ground, and which has at least one-half but not more than two-thirds of its unobstructed interior height above the average level of the ground adjacent to its exterior walls.

"ACCESSORY" is an adjective used to describe a building, structure or use. When so used, it means that the building, structure, or use has the following characteristics:

a. It is a building, structure, or use which is commonly incidental, subordinate, or secondary and exclusively devoted to the main building or structure, or the main, principal, or primary use;

b. It is located on the same lot as the main building or structure, or the main, principal or primary use; and

c. An "accessory building" shall mean a detached building not used for human habitation.

"EASEMENT" is the right to cross or use someone else's land for a specified purpose. Parties involved are often referred to as the dominant tenement (recipient of easement access from property owner) and the servient tenement (grantor of easement access/ property owner).

"RIGHT OF WAY" is the legal right, established by usage or grant, to pass along a specific route through grounds or property belonging to another. A right of way is typically related to movement from somewhere to somewhere else.

"SETBACK" means the shortest distance between a property line of a lot and the nearest part of any building, structure, excavation, or outdoor storage on a lot. ← Very important definition

Cite 7

## 1.12 Built Form and Structural Definitions (Related to Zoning Bylaw)

*""DWELLING UNIT" means a unit consisting of one or more rooms, which unit contains…"*

**The built form and structural definitions help define the shape and character of a** building or structure within the confines of the ZBL. Much like the land planning definitions, the wording within is very precise and matters very much when approaching a new development or renovation, so it has been included within the land planning section as an area of importance.

See below for these definitions, and like the land planning definitions, flip back to this section from time to time to make sure you're understanding them correctly.

### Structure Definitions

"BUILT FORM" means the function, shape, or configuration of a building.

"SINGLE DETACHED DWELLING" means a building which is freestanding, separate, and detached from other main buildings or main structures and which contains only a dwelling unit but docs not include a mobile home.

"SEMIDETACHED BUILDING" means a building containing two dwelling units, other than a duplex, with the following characteristics (89-2014):

- a. The two dwelling units are attached vertically above and below grade by a common wall at least 6m in length and at least one storey, in addition to any basement, in height;

b. Each of the two dwelling units has an independent entrance from the exterior; and

c. Each of the two dwelling units directly faces the street line.

"SEMIDETACHED DWELLING" means one of the two dwelling units constructed in a semidetached building.

"DUPLEX" means the whole of a building, which was not originally constructed as a single detached dwelling, that consists of two dwelling units, one of which has at least fifty percent (50%) of its gross floor area located wholly or partially above the other and each of which has an independent entrance either directly from the outside or through a common vestibule or hallway.

"APARTMENT BUILDING" means a building or part of a building containing three or more dwelling units, including stacked townhouses, but does not include flats, block townhouses, or street townhouse buildings. For the purpose of this definition "dwelling unit" means a unit consisting of one or more rooms, which unit contains toilet and cooking facilities.

"BED AND BREAKFAST ESTABLISHMENT" means a single detached or farm dwelling in which not more than three bedrooms are made available for the temporary accommodation of travelers, to whom meals may be furnished, but does not include a hotel or lodging house.

"BASEMENT" means that part of a building which is between two floor levels and is partly below ground, and which has at least one-half but not more than two-thirds of its unobstructed interior height above the average level of the ground adjacent to its exterior walls.

"STREET TOWNHOUSE BUILDING" means a townhouse with each dwelling unit having lot frontage and direct vehicular access to an improved street that is maintained by a municipality. Notwithstanding any other provision of this bylaw, for the purpose of this definition improved street shall have the meaning defined in Section 2 of the zoning bylaw and not the meaning defined in Article 5.13 (52-2018).

"STREET TOWNHOUSE DWELLING" means one of the dwelling units originally constructed in a street townhouse building.

"STRUCTURE" means anything that is erected, and which is fixed to or supported by the soil, a building, or another structure, but does not include a building (66-1998, 24-2014).

"STUDIO" means a building or part or part of a building used as the workplace of a photographer, craftsperson, or artist, including the instruction of art, music, dancing, languages, or similar disciplines, and may include the sale of merchandise or artifacts produced therein as an accessory use to the studio.

"STACKED TOWNHOUSE" means a building designed to contain three or more dwelling units attached side by side, two units high.

"BACK-TO-BACK TOWNHOUSE BUILDING" means a townhouse that shares a common rear wall with another townhouse for at least fifty percent (50%) of its width with each dwelling unit having lot frontage (83-2012).

"BACK-TO-BACK TOWNHOUSE DWELLING" means one of the dwelling units originally constructed in a back-to-back townhouse building.

"RETIREMENT HOME" means a residence providing accommodation primarily for persons or couples of sixty-five years of age or over where each living unit has a private bedroom, a private washroom, and separate entrance from a common hall but where common facilities for the preparation and consumption of food are provided, and where common lounges, recreation rooms, and medical care facilities may also be provided.

"PRIVATE GARAGE" means either a detached building accessory to a dwelling unit, or a part of a building which also contains a dwelling unit, designed or used for the parking or storage of vehicles of the occupants of the dwelling unit and in which there are no facilities for repairing or servicing such vehicles for gain or profit. For the purposes of this bylaw, a private garage includes a carport.

"FLAT" means a dwelling unit with the following characteristics:

   a. It is located within a building not exceeding four storeys in height, which building contains commercial uses on the first floor;
   b. If located on the first floor, a flat must be located behind the non-residential uses located at the front of the building adjacent to the street line (61-2016);

    c. It is completely separated from commercial uses; and

    d. It has an independent entrance either directly from the outside or through a common vestibule or hallway.

For the purposes of this definition, "storey" refers to storeys other than basements and the "first floor" is the floor, other than a basement, closest to the ground level (62-2000).

For the purpose of this definition, "dwelling unit" means a unit consisting of one or more rooms, which unit contains toilet and cooking facilities.

"DWELLING UNIT" means a unit consisting of one or more rooms, which unit contains toilet and cooking facilities and which is designed for use as a single housekeeping establishment. Notwithstanding the foregoing, a suite with a bedroom and bathroom but not a kitchen within a Home for the aged, nursing home, or R\retirement home shall be considered a dwelling unit for purposes of calculating density.

"CONDOMINIUM" means a building administered and maintained, or proposed to be administered and maintained, by a corporation created pursuant to the provisions of the Condominium Act.

## 1.13 Zone Definitions and Zone Symbols

*"if you're a residential investor, you're most likely to use the residential zoning definitions…"*

**Zone definitions and symbols quickly define the general use of a specific parcel,** and what can be constructed there.

Real world examples of zoning use will be given in the following chapter, so it's important to briefly see the different symbols that are available to you. Also, if you're a residential investor, you're most likely to use the residential zoning definitions. If you're a commercial investor, zones such as office, institutional, or industrial, those symbols might be better suited for your deals.

Each zone category has its own section of the zoning bylaw which outlines its requirements and opportunities respectively.

Below are some examples from the Oshawa zoning bylaw 60-94.

Like the land planning and built form definitions in previous chapters, these zoning designations are also important to note. If needed, flip back to this section from time to time to make sure you're understanding them correctly.

**Residential:**

R1 R1 Residential Zone
R2 R2 Residential Zone
R3 R3 Residential Zone
R4 R4 Residential Zone
R5 R5 Residential Zone
R6 R6 Residential Zone
R7 R7 Residential Zone
R8 R8 Residential Zone

**Office:**

SO Specialized Office Zone
OC Office Conversion Zone

**Commercial:**

CBD Central Business District Zone
PCC Planned Commercial Centre Zone
PSC Planned Strip Commercial Zone
SPC Special Purpose Commercial Zone
CC Convenience Commercial Zone
SSC Automobile Service Station Zone
HMC Hamlet Commercial Zone
HBC Harbour Commercial Zone

**Institutional:**

CIN Community Institutional Zone
MIN Major Institutional Zone

**Open Space:**

OS Open Space Zone
OSU Urban Open Space Zone
OSR Rural Open Space Zone
OSP Park Open Space Zone
OSH Hazard Lands Open Space Zone
OSE Environmentally Sensitive Open Space Zone
OSW Waterfront Open Space Zone
OSB Open Space Buffer Zone
OS-ORM Oak Ridges Moraine Open Space Zone

**Industrial**

PI Prestige Industrial Zone
SI Select Industrial Zone
GI General Industrial Zone
SPI Special Industrial Zone
HI Hamlet Industrial Zone

**Other**

AG Agricultural Zone
AP Airport Zone
UT Utilities Zone
MA Mineral Aggregate Zone
CE Cemetery Zone
UR Urban Reserve Zone
EU Existing Use Zone
SW Special Waterfront Zone
AG-ORM Oak Ridges Moraine Agricultural Zone

# 1.14 Examples of #TheHighestAndBestUse In Common Zones

*"...forested areas (woodlots), parks, golf courses..."*

**Residential- R1, R2, R5 Zones, Etc.**

**Residential land will generally have the highest and best use defined by the** parcel's location, density, zoning designation, utility servicing, and parking. These primary items dictate what a parcel may be used for (and thereby a large portion of its value), how many people can live within the boundaries of its lot lines, its current or future zoning parameters for height or setbacks, what utility capacities are available to service the building, and where the residents will put their vehicles. Uses here could be high rise towers, low rise buildings, single family homes, or similar.

**Open Space (Conservation Lands) - EP Zone**

Open space (also known as conservation lands, or environmentally protected EP) will generally have the highest and best use dictated by what is permitted to be on that land, and what ways it's allowed to be utilized. Some typical characteristics of this land would be considered farm land, flood plain, forested areas (woodlots), parks, golf courses, gardening, walking paths, natural geologic feature sites (waterfalls, tunnels, caves, creeks), driving range, sod farms. Most of these uses contain few or no permanent structures and maintain mother nature where possible.

Golf courses are a very specific example of commercial use within an environmentally protected zone. This is because the sensitive features of the land must be maintained, while giving the public a recreational use, as well as providing jobs. It's because of the zoning bylaw that major urban centers have golf courses located in nearby valleys or wetlands. If it weren't for environmental conservation, the land would be turned over to its next highest and best use which would be real estate development.

**Commercial - CI Zone**

Commercial uses will generally have the highest and best use dictated by similar nuances to that of residential uses: Location, parking, type, and size of building.

Commercial rents are typically on a price-per-square foot basis and are the major driving factor behind valuation of commercial property. Retail, restaurants, hotels, schools, and theaters are all considered commercial use and are best defined by understanding the location where that development may take place. For example, storage facilities in urban centers have fantastic utility to its patrons since high rise condo living comes with less than adequate storage space.

Conversely, storage facilities in rural areas where there is plenty of land to go around might be less attractive. The cost of construction may remain the same but the rent per square foot may diminish due to demand, dropping the value of the project. Commercial investing isn't the focus of this book, however, it is good to understand that there are many opportunities within the commercial space.

**Industrial - GI Zone**

An interesting talking point for industrial lands would be infrastructure. Transportation, utility servicing, shipping and receiving capacity, proximity to airports/bridges/major highways or nautical ports all play a factor in industrial design. #TheHighestAndBestUse for industrial design is to build what the economy directly needs to support its local workers, or be a global provider that isn't reliant on the local economy. Buildings in this regard are often purpose-constructed to their own applications and, like commercial space, not the focus of this book.

## 1.15 Compound Zoning

*"Compound zoning is commonly found in transitional neighbourhoods…"*

**Compound zoning is a unique opportunity with a given parcel of land whereby** it has multiple uses and multiple zones that it may fall under. For example, some land may be deemed single family residential but also multiunit residential. This would give the developer an opportunity to either build single-family homes or some form of apartment building. Oftentimes the compound zoning for single-family residential is less stringent than multifamily residential, and depending on the size of the land, may require the acquisition of multiple parcels in a row to meet the multifamily residential construction requirements. In cases like this, a minor variance may be an option, but the correct zoning is present and that is half the battle.

A good example of compound zoning can be found within downtown cores, where commercial space may occupy the ground floor levels/street facade, while residential uses may be permitted on the second story and above. It's situations like this which shape a city's character and provide areas for shopping, retail, dining, and transit, while allowing intensification in urban settings.

Compound zoning is also commonly found in transitional neighbourhoods where intensification initiatives are critical to the health and natural gentrification of the area. Neighbourhoods typically function in eighty-year cycles and as a neighbourhood reaches the end of this life span (unless its historic or otherwise backed by years of financial stability in affluent locations), it typically turns into the next development hot spot. This often means to tear buildings down, add more density, and start the cycle again.

Cite 7.5.

## 1.16 THE HOUSING LIFECYCLE

*"This is the final phase. Homes are older…"*

**The average life cycle of a home runs in twenty-year segments.**

*Year 1–20*
This is the "new construction" phase with shiny new windows, doors, furnaces, roof, appliances, and so on. These homes are new build, owner/investor occupied, and are on trend to "keep up with the Joneses."

*Year 21–40*
This is the "renovation phase" where homeowners notice their building is tired and needs to be updated. The roof is on its way out, the furnace broke, and the almond

coloured appliances are no longer popular. Turnover through resale is common in this phase as some people just don't want to do/facilitate the work.

*Year 41–60*
This is the second "renovation" phase. The home has been occupied by a couple different families at this point and each family has put their own spin on paint colour and handyman repairs. Some structural movement may have occurred by this point, long-term capital expenses are prevalent (brick spalling, windows/doors, weed filled gardens, roof sheathing, dated electrical panel, sagging porch, garage doors, etc.).Houses in this era may be seen as "dated" from an urban design perspective. Often extensive work is required to bring the homes back to tip-top shape, otherwise they will further deteriorate.

Year 61–80+
This is the final phase. Homes are older, some may be in the stone foundation/knob and tube era, renovations have occurred several times over the years. Major appliances and major fixtures have been traded up consistently by now, general wear and tear is high. This is the point in neighbourhoods where investors say, "Is it really worth it to fix this building, or can I swap it out for something new/more units/taller ceilings/etc.?"

In this vintage, it comes down to a function of economics, and defining the investment horizon for that owner. Compound zoning is often prevalent, and there is typically a higher and better use than a single family home.

## 1.17 Land Planning Applications

*"There are seven specific documents that any land planner must be aware of…"*

**In a simplified version of the land planning application hierarchy, a developer** would follow the following process in order to apply for a land planning application.

This is a generic version from a high level, and will change slightly depending on the geographic region you are working with. See below:

```
FEDERAL / PROVINCIAL POLICY
            ↓
    LOCAL OFFICIAL PLAN
            ↓
      ZONING BY-LAW
            ↓
  REZONING / LAND DIVISION
            ↓
       MINOR VARIANCE
            ↓
     PRE CONSULTATION
```

Cite 8.

**Land Planning Guidelines**

There are seven specific documents that any Canadian (Ontario specific) land planner must be aware of in order to have a successful land planning application completed. The level of detail of which a professional planner will comprehend these items vs. that of the average constituent looking to sever their own backyard, will vary greatly. Defining the complexity of a development application is of importance.

1. The Planning Act (Ontario) *is a large legal document that governs all provincial land planning from a high level using political framework as a guide.*

2. The Provincial Policy Statement - *Utilizing the "Planning Act," this regulates development policy and land use for the province one level deeper.*

3. The Provincial Plan - *Utilizing the "Provincial Policy Statement" and "The Planning Act," the Provincial Plan goes further in depth to touch on geographic areas of interest, transportation requirements, housing requirements, infrastructure requirements, etc.*

4. The Official Plan - *The official plan is municipality specific and with the guidance of the provincial documents noted above, it crafts the local area to what the residents and business owners most need in their communities today/for the future.*

5. Community Improvement Plans - *A local initiative that sculpts and creates incentivized redevelopment within areas needing revitalization.*

6. Local Zoning Bylaw, Development Permit, Ministers Zoning Order - *Local zoning bylaws and development permits shape the local land use and setbacks in a formalized document that is discussed in this book. A minister's zoning order (MZO) is a judgment by the Minister of Housing and municipal affairs that over rules all other planning act regulation without appeal. (Most often used in emergency situations.)*

7. Site Plan Control Bylaw - *Provides municipalities the option to control the size, shape, and characteristics of a development.*

### *Rezoning Applications*

A rezoning application is exactly the way that it reads—a government application to change land use from one designation to another. Oftentimes when you change the use, you do so to increase the future value potential in terms of density, units, setbacks, and overall site characteristics.

#TheHighestAndBestUse Quick Tip:

*Buying land on major corridors, or in areas of high-density "future use" may yield an underutilized opportunity in your town. Consider acquiring multiple smaller parcels of land where the lots can be linked to create a larger one, and then rezone that property as one big chunk. It takes a similar amount of time to rezone a large parcel, as it does a smaller infill building lot.*

Rezoning application fees vary from city to city and often range in the thousands of dollars. See the chart from the City of Toronto below that outlines their process required for any city zoning bylaw amendments, or official plan amendments. This chart is very well done and is a great visual representation on what can be achieved with the right requests.

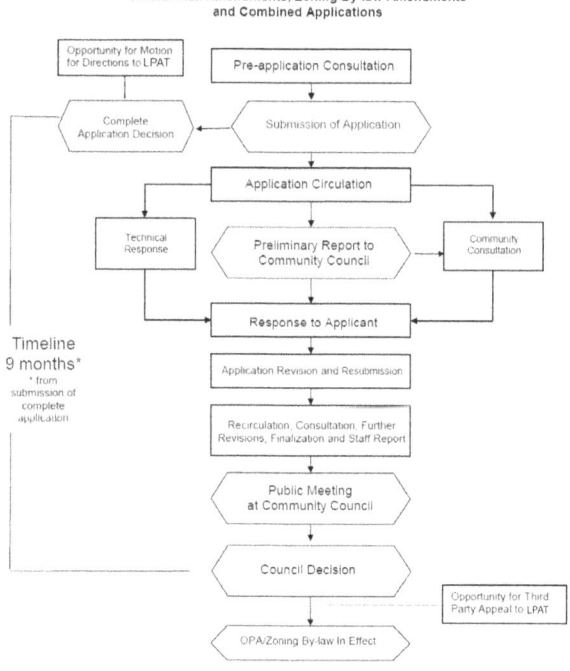

> *Cite: https://www.toronto.ca/city-government/planning-development/application-forms-fees/building-toronto-together-a-development-guide/official-plan-and-zoning-by-law-amendment/*

### *Minor Variance Applications:*

Minor variance applications relate back to the zoning bylaw and slightly modify the guidelines as to what can be constructed, and where, in a given zone. There are four tests that an applicant must ask themselves before making a minor variance request, and those four tests are as follows:

- Is the application minor in nature?
- Is it desirable for the appropriate development or use of the land, building, or structure?
- Is it in keeping with the general intent and purpose of the zoning bylaw?
- Is it in keeping with the general intent and purpose of the official plan?

Common requests on a minor variance would be items such as:

- Setbacks
- Lot coverage
- Density
- Parking
- Lot frontage
- Lot depth

*Example:*

If a developer needs 20 meters (65') of lot frontage for the creation of two lots, but the piece of land to be severed only has 19 meters of lot frontage (62.5'), this is an ideal time to request a minor variance. From a numeric perspective, 1m (3.5') split between two lots is relatively minor, and there is a good chance it would fit into the character of the existing neighbourhood. Oftentimes council members will ask the applicant questions, mainly surrounding if the request is, in fact, minor in nature and if it upholds the intent of the zoning bylaw.

One challenge an applicant may run into is that every request has its own nuances. Some cities may say, "If it's within 10% of the zoning bylaw guideline, that should be fine," whereas other cities may have less wiggle room on certain issues and more wiggle room on others. In a case such as a minor variance (or any land planning matter), I'd suggest a pre-consultation meeting to drill down on your specifics."

***Pre-Consultation Meeting:***

A pre-consultation (pre-con, for short)is a meeting with city planning staff specifically related to your subject property. Pre-consultation meetings often involve municipal planners, lawyers, engineers, consultants, and landowners to discuss pertinent issues surrounding the parcel.

These issues may include

- Severance applications
- Rezoning applications
- Dimensional constraints within a parcel
- Conservation area preservation
- Method of construction
- Construction material
- Site grading or servicing
- And many more.

A pre-consultation meeting is the lowest risk way, and least expensive way, to get written answers and solid clarity for the direction of your development before actually making a paid application to city staff.

#TheHighestAndBestUse Four Step Pre-Con Submission for DIY Submissions:

1. Call the city planner in your area, introduce yourself, and confirm they have authority to discuss the land you are considering.

2. Ask that planner what the government prefers to see for any new development in this location.(This will often refer back to the zoning bylaw, and/or the official plan.)

3. Using Step 2 as a guideline, submit a simple site plan indicating lot size, building footprint, setbacks, future plans for constructed use, and a one-page cover letter outlining your general direction.

4. Wait for comments; then adjust the site plan as needed until a formal application is required.

Note: See chapter on "How to Design Your Site Plan" for additional guidance.

#TheHighestAndBestUse Quick Tip

Some pre-cons cost money and some are at no cost to the applicant. Pay the fee if there is one, it's money well spent, as $1,000 and a few months of time upfront could save you major complications and major financial distress down the road should a formal application be rejected.

## 1.18 LAND SEVERANCE PRINCIPLES

*"General requirements within a consent application form are as follows..."*

There are two ways that a developer can sever land. The first method is a formal method called a "consent," and the second method is slight variation on that process called "part lot control."

*"Consent"*

Land division or land severance, also known as "consent," is the act of dividing an existing parcel of land into additional smaller parcels under government application and government approval. The consent process involves various facets of land planning such as:

- Formal application
- Survey and legal searches
- Zoning constraints
- Minimum lot size and minimum road frontage
- Conservation authority approval
- Municipal or regional approval
- Provincial approval
- Federal approval
- Engineering and roadway approval
- Utility servicing approval
- Zoning bylaw and minor variance amendment approval
- Emergency services approval
- Neighbourhood approval

The consent process is a formalized process where the applicant requests approval from the upper tier level of government to separate pieces of land into smaller chunks for redevelopment. This process as described above is done by way of public hearing and all local parties involved, including neighbors in the immediate vicinity, have a right to attend the hearing or make comments relating to the application. If the parcel is not on a registered plan of subdivision, a "consent" is how land gets severed.

Activities that require consent:

- Creation of limited number of lots
- Lot line adjustment

- Creation of easements or right of ways
- Land leases twenty-one years or longer

Depending on the number of lots being created, a "plan of subdivision" may be required. Plans of subdivision often require the developer to pay for infrastructure upgrades that would otherwise not be required in a formal consent process. Plans of subdivision may be required even though the parcel being divided is an interior/infill lot. Some municipalities request a plan of subdivision for as few as three or four new lots.

General requirements within a consent application form are as follows:

- Applicant information (personal or corporation)
- Type of application (consent, easement, etc.)
- Legal description
- Land details and size
- Current use/proposed use
- Agricultural information (if applicable)
- Site specific details/geographic specific details
- Zoning information
- Utility servicing information
- Studies, surveys, and engineering requirements
- Various declarations and signatures
- Environmental questionnaires

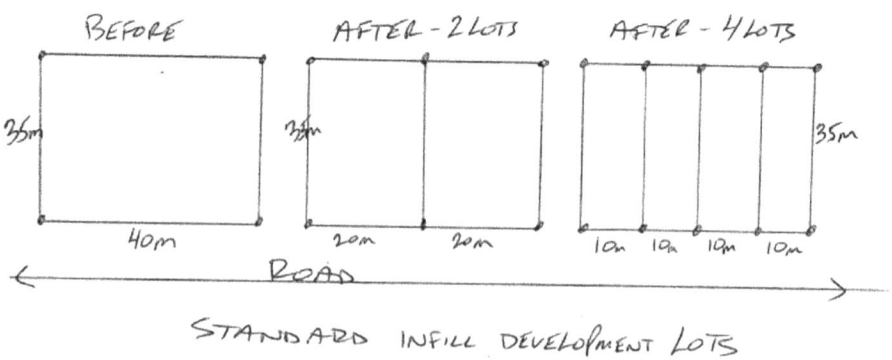

STANDARD INFILL DEVELOPMENT LOTS

> **#TheHighestAndBestUse Quick Tip: Navigable Waterways and Consent Process**
>
> *Navigable waterways are a natural land division for municipalities and are an excellent boundary for severance justification. One hundred years ago, waterway protection meant very little to the environmental agencies (If any agencies existed). Waterways were seen as a utilitarian function for industry, a place to dump trash, and somewhere for personal uses such as swimming and fishing.*
>
> *Today, these waterways are heavily regulated and the manipulation of them is highly monitored. Conservation authorities keep close eyes on the floodplain, wetlands, vegetation growth, erosion, wildlife migration, and many other areas pertaining to this.*
>
> *As a general rule, development within riparian areas are restricted, however, if a naturally formed navigable creek runs through a parcel, "consent" (formal land severance) may be granted as-of-right (by default) even in areas that do not otherwise permit the severance of land.*
>
> Cite 8.5

### *Part Lot Control*

In the Ontario Planning Act (Ontario specific), another mechanism to sever land is called "the removal of part lot control." Part lot control (PLC) is a subset of formal consent and allows municipalities to control the land severance process at a lower level of government provided the subject parcel is considered to be located on a "Registered Plan of Subdivision."

Fees and requirements are very similar (if not identical) to the "consent" process, but can sometimes be a faster way to approval because many of the decisions are made "in house" as they pertain to your file directly vs. running them up the flagpole to other levels of government.

For a part lot control application, the PLC decision must be accompanied by a public hearing so that all neighbours have a chance to voice any concerns they have about the subject lands. This public hearing is often the subject of a minor variance request during which time both the part lot control and minor variance hearings would be heard. Pending approval, the committee makes a decision.

Just like a consent or minor variance, land severances by way of PLC can be appealed to the Local Planning Appeal Tribunal (LPAT) for up to twenty days after the proposal has been approved.

> #TheHighestAndBestUse Technical How-To
>
> *PLC can be particularly helpful in instances of multiple severances occurring at the same time, where the landscape of the overall parcel doesn't change. For example, a development block of six townhouses that are situated on a registered plan of subdivision would require several "formal consent" applications in order to split the land once the units are built.*
>
> *Because a townhouse R-plan can be initially registered as one large parcel, and six units within that parcel, the PLC application can be utilized to streamline the severance process once the foundations are poured and the site specific lot lines are noted on an as-constructed survey. From that application, a bylaw would be drafted giving each townhouse a formalized legal description.*
>
> *PLC may also be used to further subdivide industrial subdivisions where common easements and parking lots are multi-utilized for several buildings on a registered plan. On an initial consent application, the largest parcel may be divided from an existing piece of land. The subject property may now potentially be further divided by PLC.*
>
> *The case law on land severances and the nuances of which method is right for your application (Formal consent vs. PLC) will be site specific.*

## 1.19 How to Read a Legal Land Description:

*"'T/W' stands for 'Together With' and 'S/T' stands for 'Subject To'…"*

As discussed in previous chapters, legal land descriptions are the building blocks for a formalized land registration process. During the Consent or PLC process, municipalities are free to dictate the way that an updated legal description is permitted to read once a land division application has been completed. Below we will discuss how this functions from a technical perspective.

These are several of the acronyms that you may find in a legal description:

- LT (Lot)
- CON (Concession)
- PCL (Parcel)
- SEC (Section)
- PT(S) (Parts)
- BLK (Block)
- PLN (Plan)
- RT (Right of Way)
- ROW (Right of Way)
- S/T (Subject To)
- T/W (Together With)
- TWP (Township)

*Severance Legal Description*

In the case of a single lot severance being split into two parcels, the legal description may convert from and to the following:

From:

"*Lot 7 of Concession 4, Township Name Here*"

To:

"*Lot 7 of Concession 4, Township Name Here* on Registered Plan xxxxx, Part 1"
"*Lot 7 of Concession 4, Township Name Here* on Registered Plan xxxxx, Part 2"

Or

LT 7, CON 4, TWN of XXX; xxRxxx Pt 1
LT 7, CON 4, TWN of XXX; xxRxxx Pt 2

What is taking place here is showing the original parcel being severed into two parcels, and the municipality is referencing a reference plan (R-plan) that shows which lot is located where. A lawyer will read the legal text and would have to reference the R-plan which is located in the land registry office. With the majority of the system being converted digitally into the land titles system, much of this can be done online.

*Easements Legal Description*

If any easements are registered on the land, it may read something like this:

"*Lot 7 of Concession 4, Township Name Here* on Registered Plan xxxxx, Part 1; T/W xxxxxx
"*Lot 7 of Concession 4, Township Name Here* on Registered Plan xxxxx, Part 2; S/T xxxxxx

What is taking place here is showing a title change in the form of an easement and how that gets registered to each parcel. For this example, the easement could be for utilities and, perhaps, one sewer pipe crosses over the other parcel of land due to geological constraint. "T/W" stands for "Together With" and "S/T" stands for "Subject To," and each of these go hand in hand.

Chapter 1.00 : #TheHighestAndBestUse of the "Land"

The parcel showcasing T/W will have easements rights over the parcel showcasing S/T, and in the event of a future sale on the property this easement will be transferred with it. Documentation regarding this easement is registered to the property title in what's called an "Instrument."

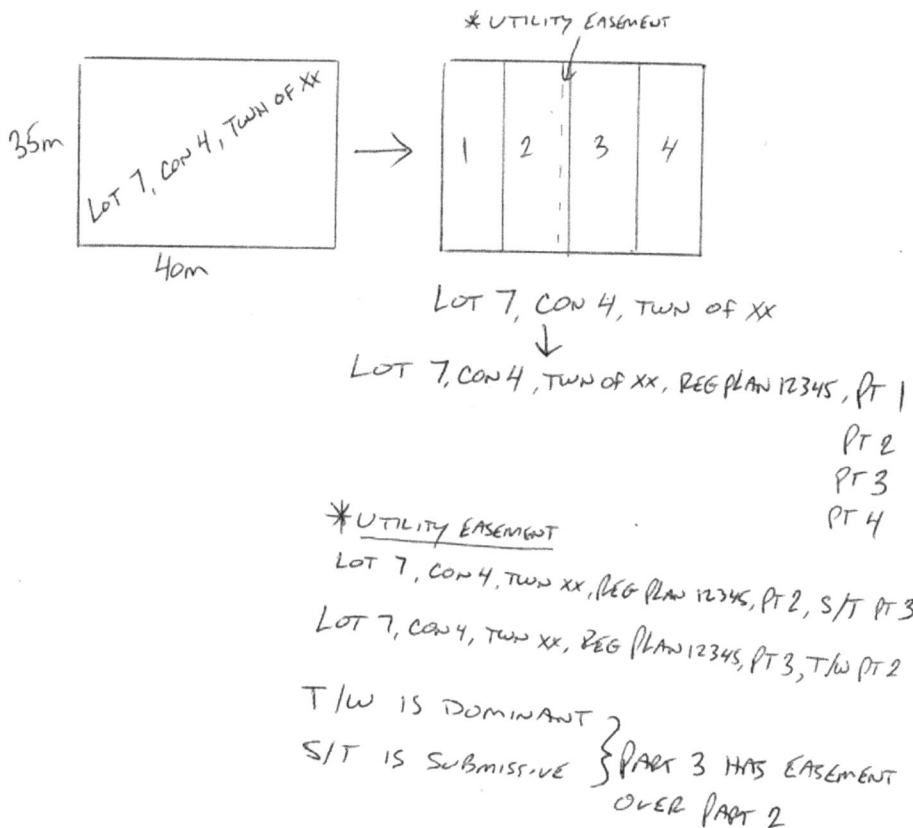

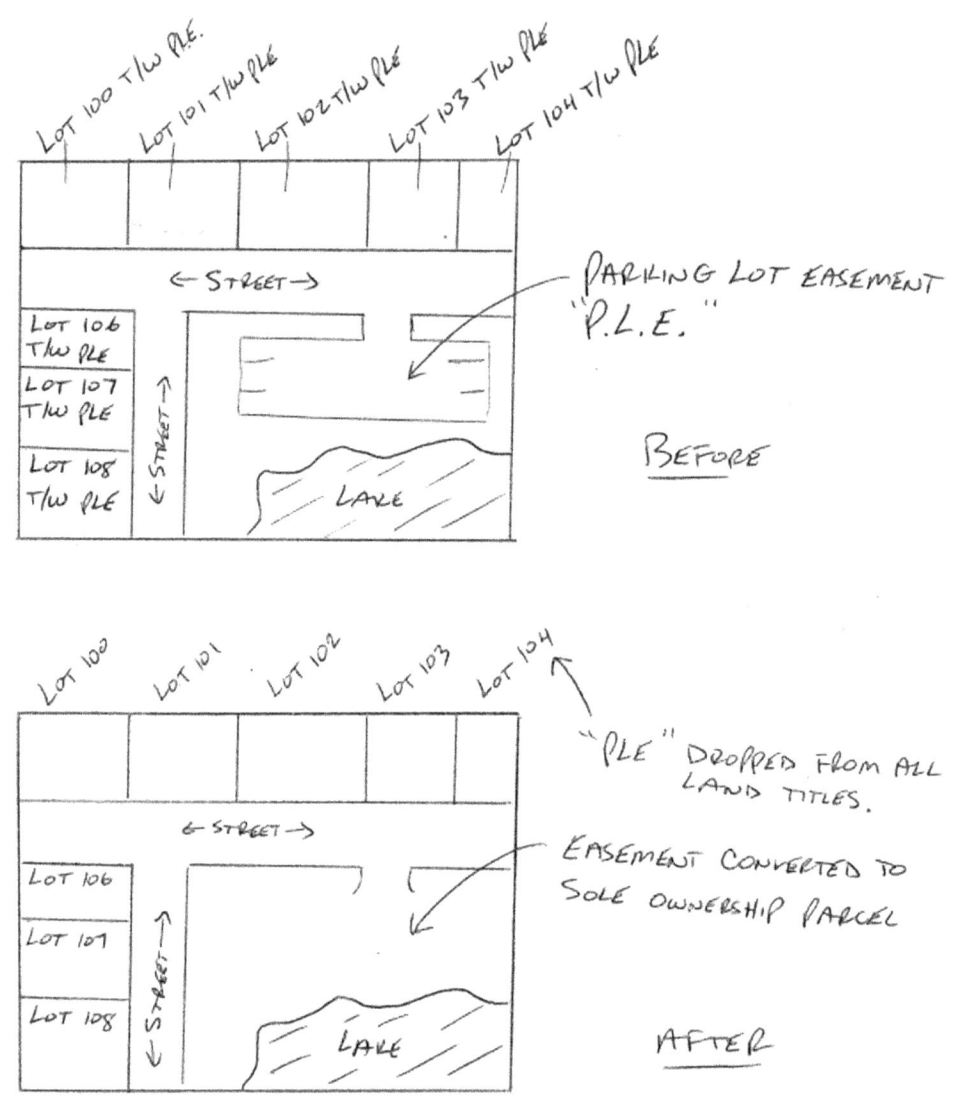

> **#TheHighestAndBestUse Story**
>
> *I once looked into a deal where several subdivision neighbours fractionally owned an easement over one parcel of waterfront land. Somewhere around the 1950s (estimated), a small community was built around a body of water, with one waterfront lot being shared amongst these multiple owners.*
>
> *Each neighbour had an easement registered on their solely owned property, which deeded them all access to use the waterfront land.*
>
> *I attempted to purchase the easement rights from all neighbours which would have allowed for a new waterfront property to be solely owned by me, and the subdivision houses to remain owned by them. After much deliberation, the odds were too low and the time required would have been too onerous for the net return once completed. I walked away from the easement opportunity but did end up purchasing a cat-lady house during the process.*
>
> *These creative strategies are what form the fundamental building blocks to unique real estate education.*
>
> Cite 9

## 1.20 Residential Building Lot Types

*"…Consider how this affects parking, access to rear yard, minor variance requirements…"*

### Interior Lot

This is the most conventional lot within a subdivision that isn't a corner lot, or cul-de-sac lot. These are often cookie cutter parcels that use their own road frontage for access, is often bordered by three neighbours (one on each side and one at the rear), and fits nicely into a city block.

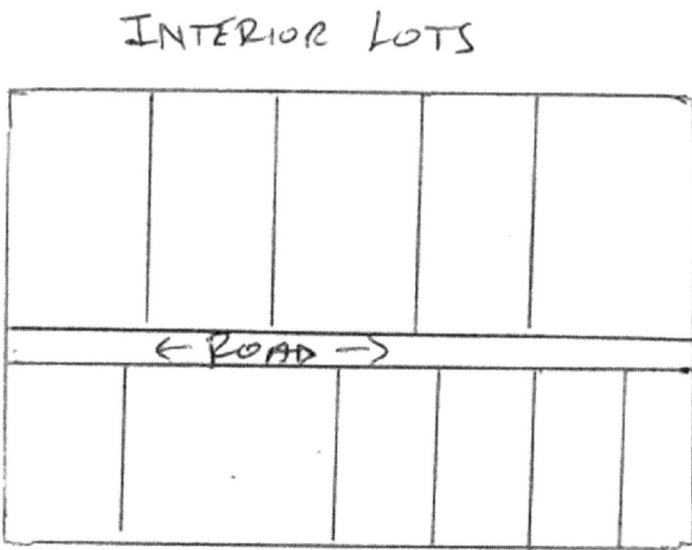

*#TheHighestAndBestUse:*
Standard infill uses apply here such as residential intensification through land severance in accordance with the local zoning bylaw. Wide lots may be severed into multiple parcels and minor variance/rezoning applications may permit additional uses or higher density.

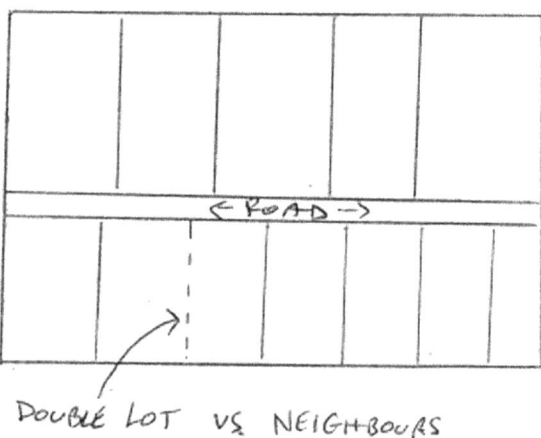

*Chapter 1.00 : #TheHighestAndBestUse of the "Land"*

## *Cul-de-Sac Lot (Court)*

These lots are situated on a roundabout style street and have a private setting by way of design. Commonly referred to as a cul-de-sac, or a "court." These lots are irregular in shape with narrow front yards and wider rear yards. The street central character of a cul-de-sac sometimes has open center-courts for kids to play or grass boulevards adding a nice feature to the surrounding land. These lots may be referred to as "Pie Shape," "Reverse Pie Shape," or "Triangular."

*#TheHighestAndBestUse:*
Reverse pie shaped lots will have a wide road frontage (great for parking) and small backyard (low maintenance), whereas a pie shape will have narrow road frontage (less parking) and larger backyard (great for pools/outbuildings).

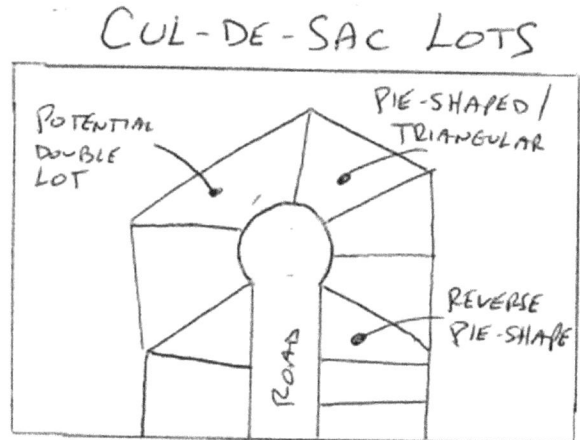

## *Corner Lots*

Also known as an exterior lot, a corner lot is situated at the corner of two adjacent streets and offers road frontage to the front yard and side/rear yard simultaneously.

*#TheHighestAndBestUse:*
In residential development, the access to rear yards may be important for additional driveways, outbuildings, garages, or coach houses. Often, an invisible "sight triangle" on the land will be owned by the governing body so vehicular traffic can

see safely around the corner while making a turn. See the definition for "sight triangle" in the "definitions" chapter.

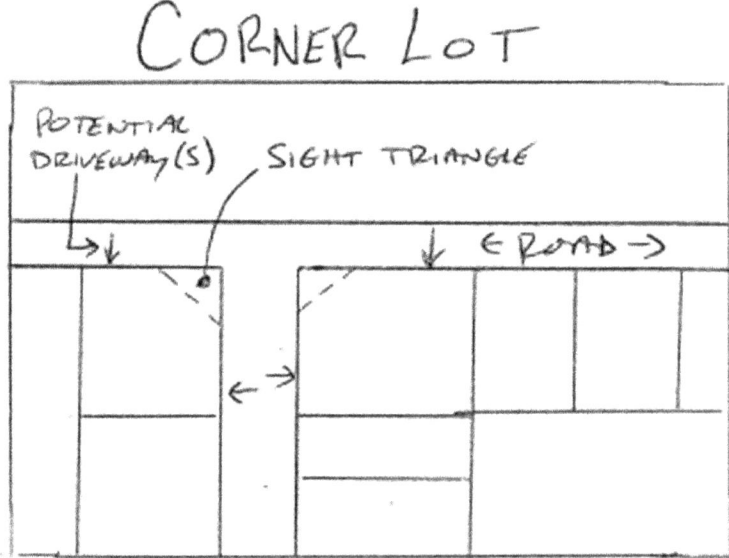

### *Key Lot/Flag Lot*

A key lot or flagpole lot are similar in nature to each other and are often described in the shape of a "key" or a standing "flag pole." These lots are typically narrow, on road frontage, with a laneway servicing a wider parcel of land behind other houses or structures. These lots lack privacy when compared to neighbouring parcels in the traditional grid system, and benefits/costs of utility servicing should be considered when planning this type of severance. However, these types of lots may unlock opportunity in existing subdivisions where economic values and intensification are a top priority.

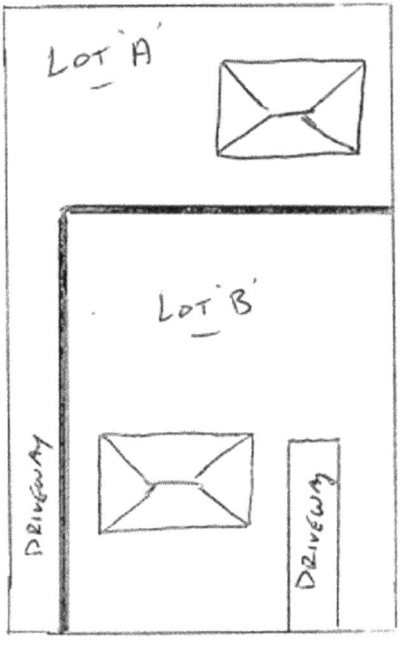 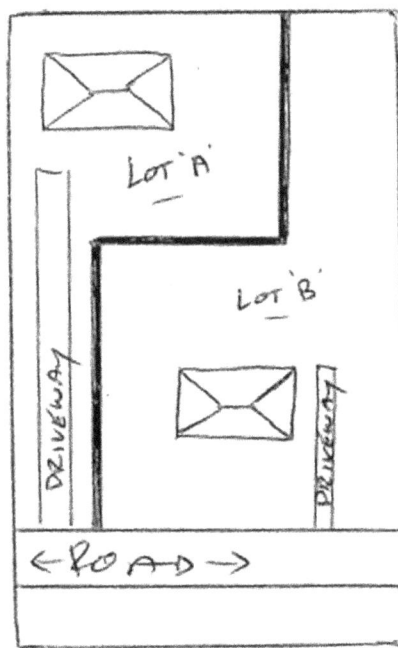

#*TheHighestAndBestUse:*

Utilizing land with site specific opportunities such as extra depth and narrow road frontage are where these lot types shine. Often, extra deep lots are underutilized for infill since human habitation only occurs within a specified periphery space around the home. For example, a 300' deep lot will underutilize the rear most 150' in most cases.

### *Regular Lots vs. Irregular Lots*

A "regular" lot is one that is perfectly symmetrical with parallel lines. An "Irregular" lot has nonparallel lines and must be measured by way of survey due to complexity.

*#TheHighestAndBestUse:*

Consider how this affects parking, access to rear yard, minor variance requirements for intensification with additional residential units, snow removal requirements, parcel specific nuances that can enhance or decrease usability, or value of the parcel.

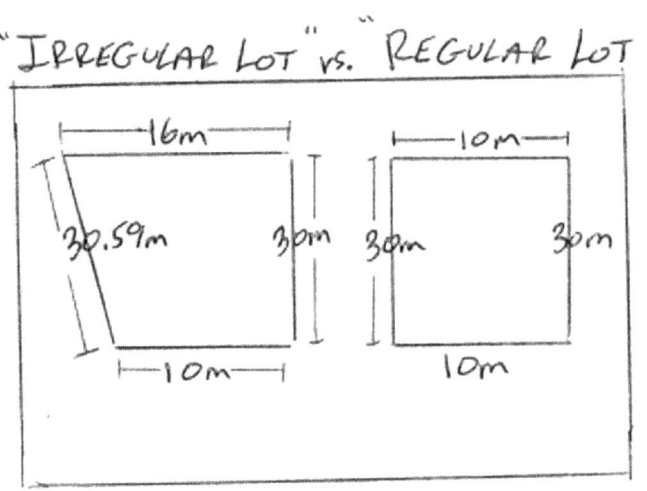

## 1.21 Legal Non-Conforming Uses

*"...Some residential examples are as follows..."*

A **"legal non-conforming"** use is often considered #TheHighestAndBestUse of the land and/or structure. Legal non-conforming (LNC), by definition, is having land or structures in legal existence that would not be granted as of today's standards either through as-of-right applications or land planning techniques ("as-of-right" means something is granted by default, without permission).

As time evolves and the needs of human habitation change, uses that existed prior to the change in zoning bylaw regulations, building code, and land planning and are considered to be "legal non-conforming," meaning they are legally allowed to continue as a permitted use although they are non-conforming to current standards.

*Some residential examples are as follows:*

- Houses built on the corner of busy intersection or built in the site triangle
- Houses built in re-designated zoning
- Houses built on extra small lots
- Houses built in flood plain/conservation lands
- Houses built on a hill without slope or subsoil studies
- Buildings with more residential units then would otherwise be permitted
- Buildings constructed using techniques that don't conform to building code but are grandfathered in
- Large buildings without elevators where elevators would now be required
- Structures built without grading plans or catch basin drainage
- Houses built too close to other setbacks without fire code retrofit
- Houses built taller or larger than current zoning permits
- Land with riparian rights (previously discussed)
- Structures serviced on existing electrical services using municipal transformers vs. requirement for dedicated transformers (apartment buildings)
- Boat house slips constructed on water where current zoning does not allow
- Cottages built on the water's edge or closer than 60' to shore
- Buildings erected without hardwired smoke detectors or monitored fire alarm systems
- Antenna or accessory use that predates a zoning bylaw change of use and may continue if unaltered
- Coach house/accessory dwelling unit structure that predates the zoning bylaw
- Multiple access points onto subject land
- Extra wide parking or lot coverage that exceeds ZBL standard

- Structures built on private laneways (common in cottage country)
- Existing uses operating in undesignated zones (example, office space in residential subdivision)
- Unregulated groundwater surrounding landfill sites
- Scrap metal and auto wrecking facilities on agricultural land
- Unregulated paint and automotive uses
- Unregulated general industrial lands for soot/smoke/smog/oil production (some newly constructed automotive buildings require an oil separator in case oil goes down the drain, and the separator shuts off to that unit until it can be pumped and sanitized)
- Seasonal dwellings using lake water vs. well water for human consumption
- Over spanned floor joists or ceiling joists
- Undersized plumbing pipes
- Etc.

#TheHighestAndBestUse

*It's common to see legal non-conforming uses in modern times. In many cases, the legal non-conforming use is legally permitted to continue if unaltered, however, if you make changes to that use there is a high likelihood that it will trigger a building code or land planning update requirement to bring it into conformity. Government regulation comes at significant cost and in many cases, if the LNC use couldn't continue the project would not be viable.*

*Example 1 - Parking*

If you have a multiunit building with one parking space per dwelling unit, and there is no land to add more parking, but you plan on adding more dwelling units, a minor variance would be needed to reduce the required parking as per the current zoning bylaw. Guest parking, lot coverage, and grading would all be taken into consideration during this request, and in a situation such as this, the landowner must be aware of the costs involved to bring the project into conformity. The efforts to add a small number of units may be cost prohibitive and #TheHighestAndBestUse remains as is.

*Example 2 - Zoning letter from a tenant*

If a property owner has a multiunit building that existed prior to a certain date set forth by a municipality (each municipality is different), provided significant proof of existence previous to that date is available, oftentimes the multiunit building will be considered legal non-conforming and may continue its use. In a best efforts approach for residential financing, this zoning approval letter from a seller is worth its weight in gold.

I had completed a multi-residential property of which a tenant had lived in the same unit for almost thirty years. Upon purchase, the previous landowner was able to secure a letter from this tenant outlining her tenancy duration, which I then provided to the zoning officer for a legal non-conforming status letter. This secured the residential financing I needed to refinance the building after the renovation, allowed me to create housing, and brought the building into zoning compliance.

## 1.22 The Local Planning Appeal Tribunal (LPAT)

*"Originally Named the Ontario Railway and Municipal Board (ORMB)…"*

In brief, the local planning appeal tribunal (LPAT) is an Ontario governing body that resolves disputes between applicants (typically developers) and governments who have denied land planning applications.

Each province has their own form of land planning appeal court, of which are similar in nature to the Ontario LPAT.

The below information is cited from the LPAT website—they really say it best.

*What is the LPAT?*
"The Local Planning Appeal Tribunal (LPAT) is an adjudicative tribunal that hears cases in relation to a range of land use matters, heritage conservation, and municipal governance. Appeals that come before LPAT are identified through policies found in the Planning Act, Aggregate Act, Heritage Act, Municipal Act, Development Charges Act, and Expropriations Act. These include matters such as official plans, zoning bylaws, subdivision plans, consents and minor variances, land compensations, development charges, electoral ward boundaries, municipal finances, aggregate resources, and other issues assigned by numerous Ontario statutes."

*LPAT History and the OMB*
"LPAT was formerly known as the Ontario Municipal Board (OMB). The OMB was an independent adjudicative tribunal that conducted hearings and made decisions on land use planning issues and other matters. The OMB was also Ontario's first independent, quasi-judicial administrative tribunal. Originally named the Ontario Railway and Municipal Board (ORMB), the ORMB oversaw municipalities' accounts and supervised the rapidly growing rail transportation system among municipalities. In 1906, the ORMB assumed new responsibilities, including those previously carried out by the Office of the Provincial Municipal Auditor, and was renamed to the OMB in 1932."

*Various Policy Acts that the LPAT Represents*

- "The Planning Act governs land use planning and development in the province of Ontario. LPAT may hear appeals based on the decisions of single tier, lower tier, upper tier municipal governments. The act sets out who is eligible to make an appeal to LPAT, and the procedures that must be followed to do so."

- "The Aggregate Resources Act provides for the standards and policies that aggregate and petroleum industries must comply with. The act aims to ensure long-term management of resources and reduces negative impacts on the public. LPAT may hear objections or referrals of license applications."

- "The Development Charges Act, 1997 grants municipalities the right to impose charges on property owners when developing or redeveloping land. The fees charged are to help pay for new services and infrastructure needed for growth. The act also provides for education development charges."

- "The Expropriations Act provides for a means for those expropriated to receive fair compensation when their lands are expropriated or affected by nearby expropriation. It also sets out the authority and process that must be followed in order to expropriate."

- "The Consolidated Hearings Act provides a streamlined hearing process for municipal, private, and provincial projects or proposed activities that might otherwise require hearings by more than one tribunal or files that fall under one or more pieces of legislation."

- "The Environmental Assessment Act is an example of legislation that LPAT deals with under the Consolidated Hearings Act (by way of a joint board with members of the Environmental Review Tribunal)."

- "The Ontario Heritage Act gives municipalities and the provincial government powers to preserve the heritage of Ontario. The primary focus of the act is the protection of heritage buildings, cultural heritage, natural landscapes, and archaeological sites. LPAT hears appeals of certain municipal decisions related to heritage preservation."

You can find more information on the LPAT here: https://olt.gov.on.ca/tribunals/lpat/about-lpat/

## 1.23 Studies, Surveys, Engineered Documentation

*"If you are building on or near an arterial road such as a major thruway…"*

### Survey

**A survey is a legal document that outlines the boundaries of your piece of land** and all structures upon it. It will outline the dimensions of all lot lines, the setback distances of structures to those lot lines, and will locate the geographic area/title of the land for registration purposes. Prior to the advent of title insurance, a survey was commonly used to transfer title when buying or selling real estate. Since the advent of title insurance, surveys have become less common in the daily transactions and maintain their prevalence in the development space.

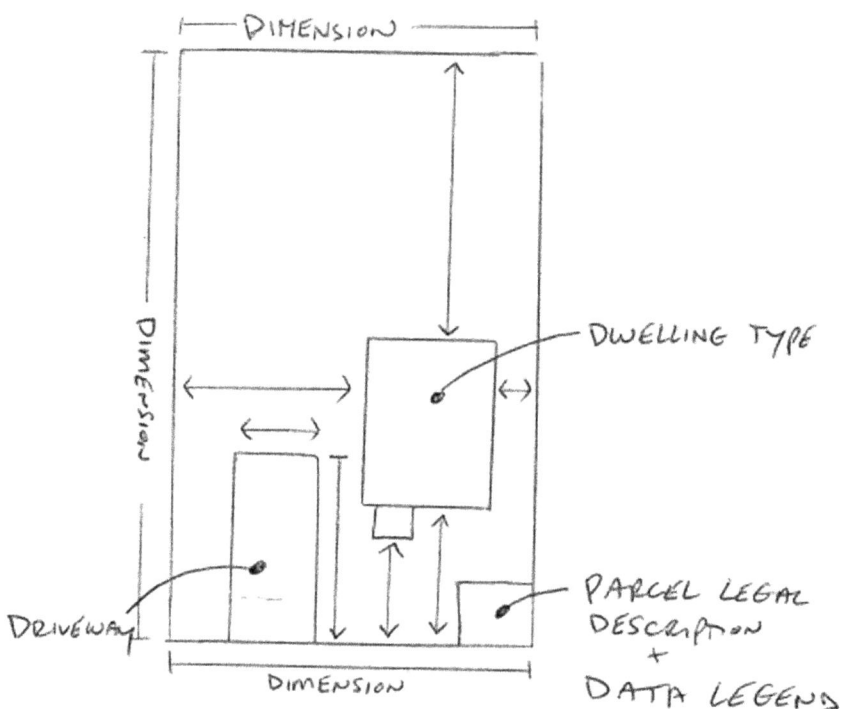

### Reference Plan

A reference plan is a document that outlines the boundary of your parcel, its length of lot lines, its boundaries vs. that of your neighbour, and also the legal description of the land within the subdivision it was built.

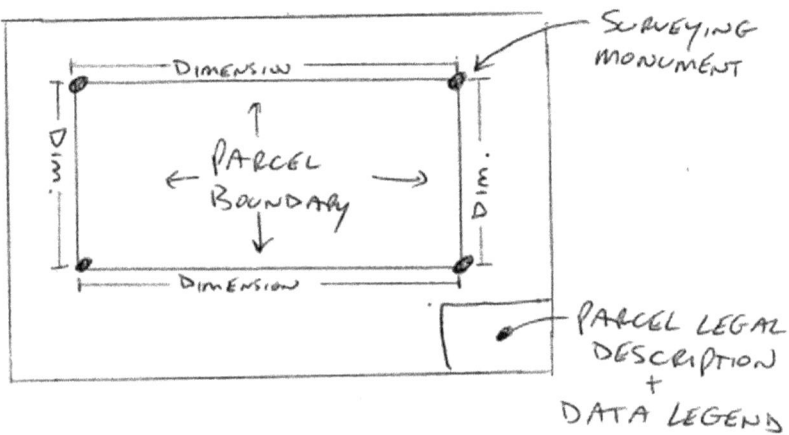

## Plan of Subdivision

A plan of subdivision is very similar to a reference plan, and generally refers to a plot of land within the underlying fabric of a subdivision. For example, in Ontario, Canada, a reference plan will refer to a plan of subdivision for items such as severance. When making planning applications for multiple lots (typically three or more lots), you are creating a subdivision. Subdividing land into several parts can be a more laborious task than a single severance of one lot into two because, as the saying goes, "Growth pays for growth." This rule applies to new land and forces new requirements onto the developer such as sidewalks, boulevard trees, improved roads, utility infrastructure, etc.

## Grading Plan and Topographic Survey

A grading plan is a legal document that engineers the slope of the land within your property boundaries. Slope (grading) is typically for control of overland water such as rain or snow, as well as soil condition control for geologic movement. For any new construction or site modifications, a grading plan is required to show where the water will be directed and if pooling will occur. Building on the side of a cliff, near wetlands, in areas of impervious soil, or areas with a high asphalt requirement would have an impact on the grading plan.

The topographic survey uses data from survey and reference plan to generate the existing lay of the land as it currently sits. On a "topo," it will identify structures, vegetation of any physical significance (trees, bushes, gardens), well heads, septic tank lids, etc.

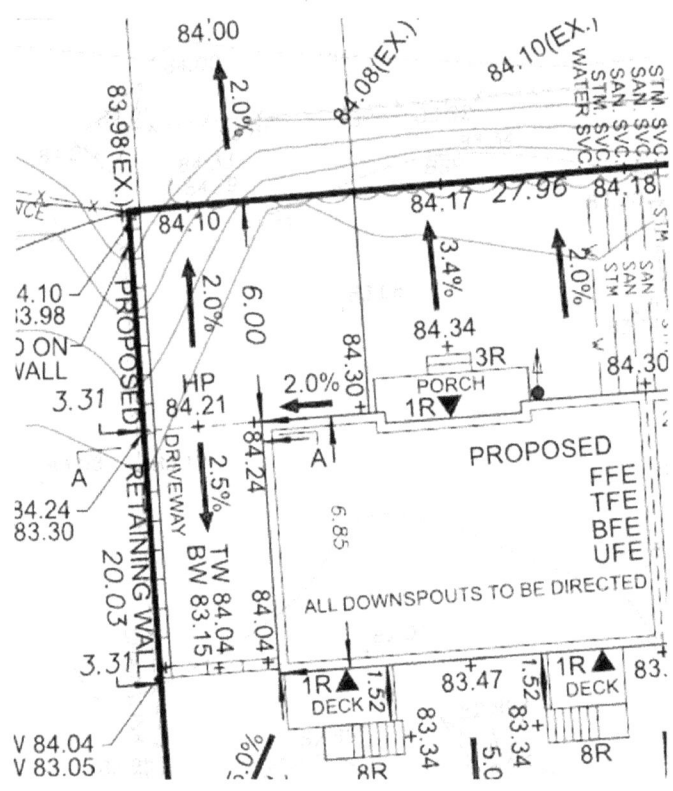

**Tree Study**

Depending on the jurisdiction, a tree study may be required in order to preserve or remove existing vegetation. During the course of a development proposal or building permit, oftentimes a tree that was previously utilized to create shade in a backyard or add character to a street facade may need to be removed. Some cities are very particular on any manipulation of the municipal canopy and have bylaws in place to prevent, restrict, or outright prohibit any changes in this regard. A tree study may be undertaken to discuss what species of tree is being dealt with, what the ramifications of that tree may be on surrounding trees or habitat, and if the tree must be preserved or if it can be removed. This type of study goes by many names, but most commonly "Tree Preservation Study" or "Arborist Report" are the most accurate.

## Wildlife Studies/Bird Migration Study

Wildlife and bird migratory patterns are a common study required when constructing tall buildings in a wind vane or structures close to environmentally significant lands such as EP, conservation, wetland, and waterways. These studies evaluate the type of animals in the local vicinity, the birds that fly in the direction of your proposal, and how the proposal may impact the natural habitat of them. These studies may be seasonal, so careful planning must be done to reduce any impact on your development timeline. An example here may be a fishery habitat, and if your proposed bridge or causeway development impacts a creek or riverbed where fish spawn, this may be restricted to spring months. Historical data may be of benefit in this scenario.

## Archaeological Report

An archaeological report is a subsoil and historical document that pertains to any prior land use as far back as can be dated. Indigenous burial sites are a prime example of this, and any artifacts found during a subsoil sampling will need to be examined by the governing officials for authenticity and significance. In some cases, shovel excavation to a shallow digging depth is all that is required, with the soil samples being sifted onsite. In other cases, most notably where historical evidence or onsite conditions require the additional efforts, machine excavation may occur. These costs are typically the responsibility of the developer.

## Environmental Site Assessments

An environmental site assessment (ESA) is commonly a three stage process, with phase one being least invasive and primarily a historical search and visual inspection, and phases two and three being more invasive.

A phase one ESA involves a background check on the property, it's prior land use, and prior uses surrounding the adjacent properties. If your property was always residential, but the neighbouring property was or is a gas station, you can be certain that further steps in your environmental clearance will be required. Oftentimes it's not the current land use that is in question, it's what took place 100 years ago when there were no rules against contamination and the public took an "anything goes" approach to subsoil conditions.

A phase two ESA typically involves drilling subsoil bore holes in the dirt to examine what may be taking place at various elevations underground. The boring machine will provide these samples to the engineer for examination, and these examinations may include soil type, soil mix, hydrocarbon evaluation, heavy metals, or acid tests, etc.

A phase three ESA will be the remediation phases pending results of the phase two ESA. If the phase two study returns results that are below the contamination limits, no further action may be required. If the soil comes back hot, then remediation is required. Remediation involves excavation of the soil to a set digging depth prescribed by the environmental engineer. A gas station may have a different digging depth than a residential site because residential (consumer) waste might be mainly topical in nature, whereas a leaky buried fuel tank (commercial) might have been leaking for a long time. As a general rule, a residential site will be the most highly scrutinized and must have better soil than a commercial use site being replaced by another commercial use site.

**Noise Study**

If you are building on or near an arterial road such as a major thruway, large highway, a high impact intersection, or near commercial uses, a noise study may be required. The noise study is typically registered on the title of a property when completed and outlines for a potential buyer and how the noise may impact their reasonable enjoyment of the subject lands. The noise study will also impact the construction of the home and may force the use of sound batt insulation in walls where standard fiberglass batt or spray foam may have been appropriate. A noise study may also require the installation of air conditioning as part of building permit approval.

**Traffic/Parking Study**

A traffic study is undertaken by an engineer to measure the flow of vehicles down a particular corridor and assess the traffic flow impact on adjacent developments.

Sometimes this is undertaken at the government level to understand specific characteristics of movement, and sometimes it is done by the developer for site specific purposes. Common uses here would be roadway construction justification and public transit requirements.

A parking study may also be completed by the government or developer to better understand the needs for parking and how they may impact a city or site specific issue. Government interest examples may be seen as understanding the street parking capacity in a downtown core or if a parking garage is required. Developer interests would be related to site specific requirements such as building more units than parking capacity would otherwise allow.

**Planning Justification Report**

A planning justification report, PJR, is a report that is generated by a registered planning professional (RPP) to justify "for" or "against" a development proposal. This is a lengthy document that outlines several items such as: Site description and history, surrounding land uses, official plan policy, site specific zoning, traffic and public transit, urban design, geological constraints, site plan discussion, and many more. For smaller infill developments, this may be a straightforward process. For larger developments, this is a very extensive process.

## 1.24 UTILITY INFRASTRUCTURE:

*"In older residential developments, groundwater, and sewage water..."*

Public utility infrastructure on a development site can be an expensive and time-consuming undertaking. Major utility services would include:

- Telephone,
- Natural gas
- Hydro
- Cable

- Municipal water supply
- Sanitary sewer connections
- Storm sewer connection

Moving forward, we may start seeing fiber optics or other communication lines becoming standard install for infill projects as is being done on newer subdivisions already.

During the planning phase, or even during the pre-consultation meeting, a developer should find out from the development approvals officer what you will be required to string into the build site. At this point, you will need to determine if certain infrastructure must run underground or overhead.

### *Overhead Utilities*

Overhead utilities would be limited to hydroelectric and communications. Utilities like electrical services have been run overhead for hundreds of years using wood, concrete, and fiberglass poles. Commonly referred to as a "hydro pole" or a "telephone pole." These poles often carry services for electricity, as well as communications like telephone and TV cable at the same time. The owner of that pole may actively lease a portion of it to another party. If you've ever wondered why poles are in municipal right of ways, and why the government often owns the boulevard in front of your home, this is a prime example.

Hydro from an overhead pole is often fed to homes and businesses directly through the use of a "pole transformer" or "pole pig." These transformers are the large grey cylindrical devices that hang from the pole and convert high voltage transmission line electricity into lower voltage household or business electricity commonly known as 110v or 220v.

### Underground Utilities

*Electrical*

On the topic of electricity, this can also be run underground. In newer subdivisions, larger commercial buildings and institutional buildings, the electrical services are run underground to clean up the visual appeal of an area and to provide lower maintenance to the line crews. In a commercial area, trucks and busses may contact the lines posing a health and safety risk, and in a subdivision the lines cause visual distraction and reduce the esthetics of a neighbourhood.

At one time, overhead lines were run along the rear of a property in effort to promote a cleaner curb appeal but eventually just went underground. These underground service lines are often fed by "Pad Mount transformers" that you will see along the boulevard. These transformers are large and encased with steel or fencing, and in some cases have been painted to look like trees, bushes, and architecture. One downside of underground hydro is that if/when maintenance is required, it is very expensive and requires excavation.

*Water/Sanitary Sewer/Storm Sewer*
Public water, sanitary sewer, and storm sewer is another common underground utility service provided by the governing body to service a development proposal. Starting with public water, this is fed from a main line under the roadway and into the building. It's common that the utility company stops their provided services at the property line, and it's up to the developer to service their build site as required. At this connection, there is often a "water box" situated on the boundary between municipally owned property and privately owned property. This water box may be an indication of your actual front lot line if it was placed in the right location when installed and is the valve that controls water flow into your structure. In retrofit applications where municipal water is piped into rural areas, the pipes may be laid at any time underneath or alongside a municipal roadway, eliminating the need to use a water well.

Sanitary sewers, also known as "sani," serve the function of carrying waste water from the structure and into the municipal system for filtration. In many residential uses, a 4" to 6" sewer pipe services this underground utility up to the property line, after which the developer must direct the pipe into the appropriate area for hookup. A large difference between water service and sewer service is that sewers require proper slope to function and is a non-pressurized system. The sewer waste only flows downhill with appropriate slope, whereas a water supply is considered pressurized and can run uphill in any direction. Careful planning on a development must be undertaken to ensure the depth of the municipal sewer is lower than the outflow pipe in the structure to be built. An example would be a basement that is dug too deep, where the sewer pipe is higher than the basement bathroom. In situations like this, a sewage ejector must be used to get waste water to a higher point prior to the gravity feed system taking over.

Storm sewers, also known as "storm," function in a similar way to sanitary sewers in the sense that it carries water away from the house using a gravity fed sloping pipe. However, a storm connection will connect the foundation weeping system of the building to pick up groundwater at the foundations base, and carry that water to the storm sewer mainline, not sewage. The storm sewer mainline is often an unfiltered pipe that heads directly to a lake or rudimentary silt bed, which is then dispersed in an area that won't affect human habitation.

Storm sewers can sometimes be replaced with sump pump discharge systems. In older communities where storm sewers may not exist (oftentimes when there is no curb separating the municipal roadway from the front lawn in a subdivision), sump pump ejectors must be used to discharge the groundwater from the foundation walls and back up to surface level for redistribution in the grass. On commercial projects, the sump pump option is typically less viable because of the solid surfaces like parking lots or concrete infrastructure and thus nowhere for the water to re-penetrate into the soil.

In older residential developments, groundwater and sewage water (sani and storm) were connected to the same outflow pipe, which from a functioning perspective would work. However, the challenge for municipal servicing department was that they had to filter the sewage waste as normal, in addition to the previously uncontaminated groundwater. The requirement for extra capacity places strain on a system that doesn't need to exist, and the systems were separated.

**Private Utilities**

Private utility infrastructure is separate from public utility infrastructure. Private utilities may include sprinkler systems, underground storage tanks (USTs for oil or heat related), drinking water wells (dug, bored, or drilled), garden electrical wires/plumbing, septic sewer installation (septic tank and weeping bed), sewage holding tank, electrical conduits to outbuildings, such as a garage/shed/wood-fired heat house, etc.

*Well and Septic*
Well systems and septic systems will be the most common form of private utilities in the residential space so we will mention them here. Water well systems can be dug, drilled, or bored, and range from 20–500' in depth.

A dug well is often found with 4' wide concrete casings that can be seen above grade. These wells are cavernous in nature and typically stop around 40–60' in depth. A well pump may sit in the bottom of the well (submersible pump) or inside the house (jet pump).

A drilled well is installed with a drilling rig and steel well casing anywhere from 20'–500' in depth and is the more expensive option since well drillers charge on a per linear-foot basis. A drilled well pump sits at the bottom of the well casing and pumps water up to the point of use, rather than a pump inside a utility room sucking water from the hole. The drilled well system is the most versatile and can be installed through a wide range of subsoil conditions, including bedrock.

Septic systems consist of two parts: A large, baffled tank and weeping bed. The baffled tank collects waste discharge from bathrooms, cooking and bathing facilities, separates the solids from the liquids, and then allows the liquids to pass through to the weeping bed. While the solids are decomposing naturally, the liquids go into the soil through a series of pipes and drainage areas.

Specifically relating to zoning and setbacks, there is a minimum distance between a well and septic system to maintain safe drinking water for the occupants of a structure. Commonly, the setback required from a septic system to dug well is 100m and 50m to a drilled well. This setback also relates to neighbouring wells, not just your own, as contamination can occur over invisible property line boundaries. Septic systems must also have setbacks to property lines as per zoning on the property. Reduced footprint systems are available for small lot parcel applications.

# 1.25 How to Start Designing Your Site Plan

*"Good deals are found, great deals are created." ~Rae Ostrander*

**This is one of the areas where education, taking action, and using some creativity** come into play. Now that we have some fundamentals behind land development in our tool pouch we can look at the ZBL in greater detail to see what types of restrictions we have for a given type of built form.

In the upcoming chart there are two notable areas for discussion. The "residential type" being the type of structure we are looking to build (single detached, semi detached, etc.) and the numeric columns below that, outlining data relating to that structure and its location upon the land.

For the purposes of this example, we will plan #TheHighestAndBestUse of this land for a single detached dwelling on an interior lot measuring 9m x 35m in the R2 zone. (City of Oshawa, ZBL 60-94.)

- 7.3 -

Table 7.2 – Regulations for R2 Zones

| Residential Type | Single Detached Dwelling | Semi-Detached Building on a Corner Lot | Semi-Detached Building on Interior Lot | Semi-Detached Dwelling on Corner Lot | Semi-Detached Dwelling on Interior Lot | Duplex |
|---|---|---|---|---|---|---|
| Minimum Lot Frontage(m) | 9.0 | 21.0 | 18.0 | 12.0 | 9.0 | 12.0 |
| Minimum Lot Area ($m^2$) | 270 | 595 | 550 | 320 | 275 | 450 |
| Minimum Front Yard Depth (m) | 6.0 | 6.0 | 6.0 | 6.0 | 6.0 | 6.0 |
| Minimum Interior Side Yard Depth (m) | for interior lots, 1.2m on one side only, and for corner lots 0.0m, provided however that, for both interior and corner lots, in no case shall the distance between dwelling units be less than 1.2m | 1.2 | 1.2 | 0.0 | 1.2 on one side only | 1.2 |
| Minimum Exterior Side Yard Depth(m) | 2.4 | 2.4 | N/A | 2.4 | N/A | 2.4 |
| Minimum Rear Yard Depth (m) | 7.5 | 7.5 | 7.5 | 7.5 | 7.5 | 7.5 |
| Maximum Lot Coverage (%) | 40 | 40 | 40 | 40 | 40 | 40 |
| Maximum Height (m) | 9.0 | 9.0 | 9.0 | 9.0 | 9.0 | 9.0 |

(62-2000, 89-2014)

City of Oshawa Zoning By-law Number 60-94

To clarify that you are reading the chart correctly, to build a single detached dwelling in the R2 zone for this city, we need:

- A minimum lot frontage of 9 m
- A minimum lot area of 270 square meters
- A minimum front yard depth of 6 m
- Etc.

Note: When planning your building envelope, it's important to understand that when mapping out this location for your new building, the most restrictive measurement applies to your zoning parameters. For example, if the building is slightly angled on the lot and one corner of the building is 1.3m setback and the other is 1.1m setback, the 1.1m setback applies.

*Seven Steps to Creating a Simple Site Plan:*

1. Visualize your build site, document the frontage, depth, and overall lot area. In this case, 9m frontage, 35m depth, and overall lot area of 315 square meters.

2. Within the build site, draw lines to outline your setback restrictions on each side yard, rear yard, and front yard setbacks. In our case, 1.2m side yard setbacks, 7.5m rear yard setback, and 6m front yard.

3. Consider your parking requirement. For this example, we will use a standard parking space of 2.75m wide x 5.5m deep. Mark this on the plan as well. Most single family homes require two parking spaces, and the parking location is typically determined by the ZBL and the existing character of the neighbourhood.

4. You now have a rectangular building envelope in which you can position your building. Calculate the size of this. In our case, it's 5.05m wide x 21.5m long (108.57 square meters).

5. Calculate the total lot coverage, 108.57sm building envelope/315sm overall lot size. Total = 34.4%.

6. Compare notes with the regulations vs. what you've designed. In our example, we meet the minimum lot size, we meet all minimum setbacks, and we are lower than the maximum permitted lot coverage.

7. Submit for pre-consultation and site plan approvals, or continue on to interior floor plans now that the exterior footprint has been confirmed.

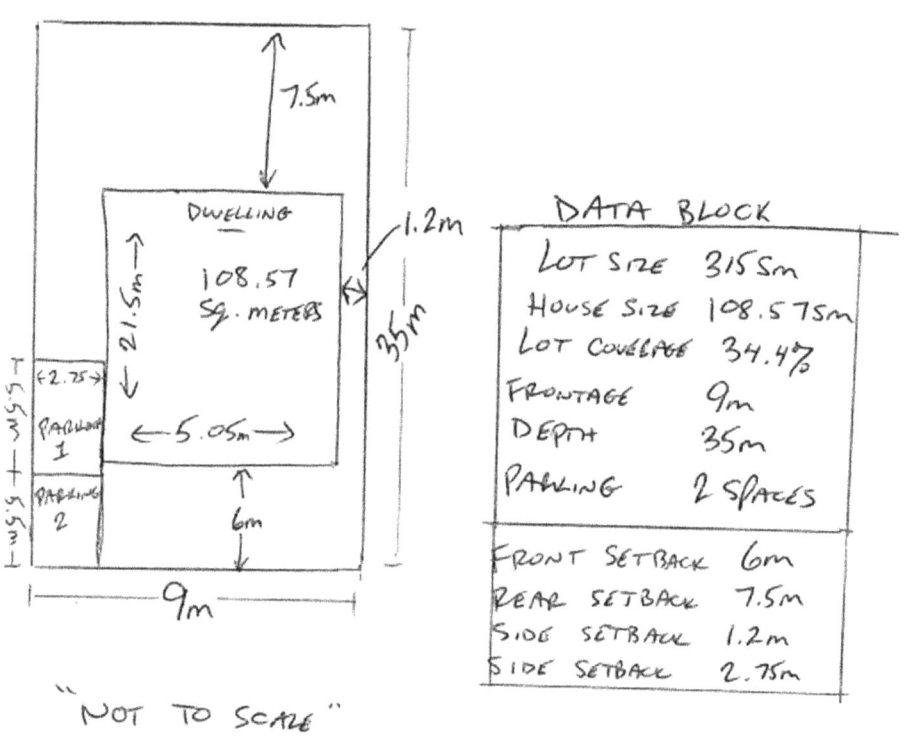

Note: This has been overly simplified to get the ball rolling. If these steps are outside of your comfort zone, hiring an urban planner to help you here is always an option. Urban planners are familiar with site plans, zoning regulations, and land use.

#TheHighestAndBestUse

As you can see for a semidetached building or duplex, even though we are in the same zoning designation, each of those defined housing types have different requirements for the land use depending on what is benign built. This is why the zoning and setbacks are so important because it dictates exactly how large we can build and where that building can be placed.

In a smaller infill site, these restrictions can become onerous when the lot size is smaller than the ZBL typically permits. This is where the minor variance and/or rezoning applications come into play.

> *Often, but not always:*
>
> - *The more density that you can get on a piece of land, the more it's worth.*
> - *The bigger the building you can get on a piece of land, the more it's worth.*
> - *The more titles you can create through land severance, the more it's worth.*
> - *There is an economic dead zone between five- and fifteen-unit buildings where the expenses of development/construction outpace the additional value created.*
>
> *#TheHighestAndBestUse starts from the ground up. The first place money is made is on the land.*

# 1.26 Real World Land Planning Stories

*"What's the upside potential and what's the downside risk?"*

### 1.24a The Semi detached Severance

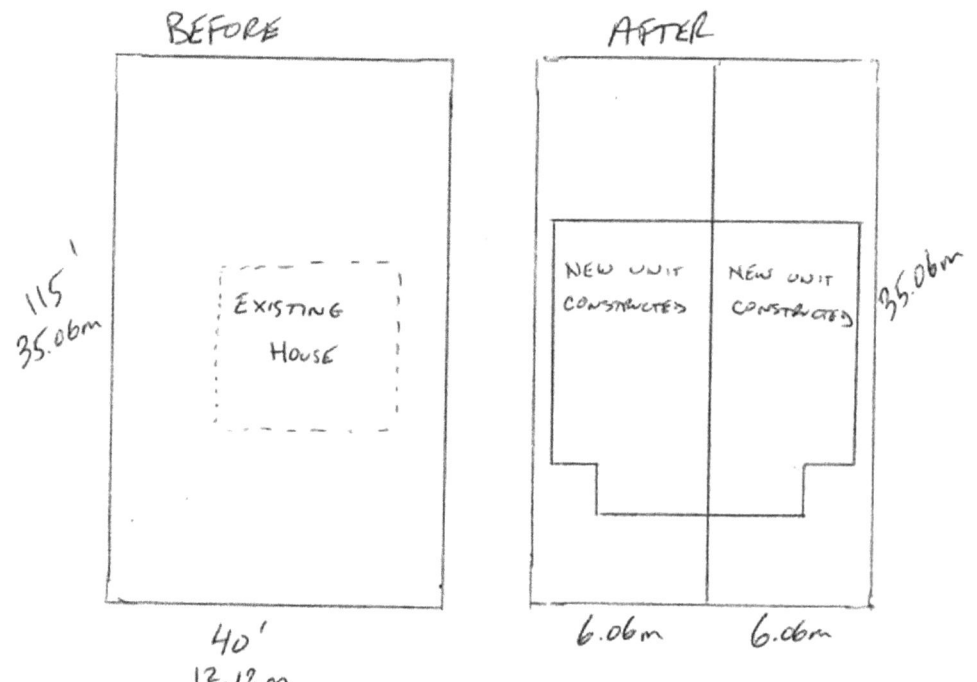

On a recent development deal I completed, I took a piece of land that was 40' (12.12m) wide and cut it down the middle to create 2–20' lots. This piece of land was 115' (35.06m) deep and had preferential zoning for semi detached homes. This meant that I could take the bungalow that was on the land, create two 20' (6.06m) wide lots, legally sever the property, and have two titles upon completion.

The process that I took to evaluate this piece of property was fairly straightforward: purchase it at a price that made sense "as is" and under the current use, so that if my high-flying plans of redevelopment didn't work out, I would still be okay.

I am a big believer in always asking myself, "What's the upside potential and what's the downside risk." The upside potential was having two houses instead of one, and the downside risk was not being able to get approvals and being stuck with a junky fixer upper. So in this case, I made an offer based on what I felt was fair and the seller accepted. The negotiation was fairly straightforward and the deal was quick. I closed on the property and soon began the development.

My next steps were to apply for a minor variance because the property itself wasn't quite wide enough, as per the zoning bylaw regulations, to fit two houses. Functionally, the site works, but as per the zoning bylaw it was not permitted. So I made my application and paid the fees. Before the waiting game began for my council hearing, I had a meeting with a municipal planner and told them what I was hoping to do. From this meeting, I had a preliminary go ahead so I knew that what I was proposing wasn't completely out of line and still fit within the criteria that the government wanted to see.

My hearing came, I sat in front of council and told them my plans, and the plans were approved conditionally on what was called "architectural control." Architectural control is a fancy way of saying that the government will tell you how this whole development should look once it's built so that it conforms with the neighbourhood. To me it made sense, the requests were fairly minimal, and I'm all about being fair so we moved forward with the process. With the technicalities out of the way, I now knew that each title would be construction-ready land, and whatever I was able to put on that land in terms of a beautifully designed building would only enhance that value when it was complete.

### #TheHighestAndBestUse Key Takeaways from Story:

- *Plan based on downside risk and hope for upside potential.*
- *Generally, more titles = more value.*
- *Land value is based on use and zoning.*
- *Pre-consultation meetings are extremely valuable.*
- *Always know what you can build "as of right"—always.*

### *1.24b Point Roberts, Washington: A Political Real Estate Play*

Point Roberts, Washington is a geographic area situated on the southern tip of Vancouver, British Columbia. The tiny region is ever so slightly south of the 49th Parallel (Canada/USA border), which means as-of-right it is to be considered American soil, although it's largely connected to Canada and could almost, practically, be called Canadian.

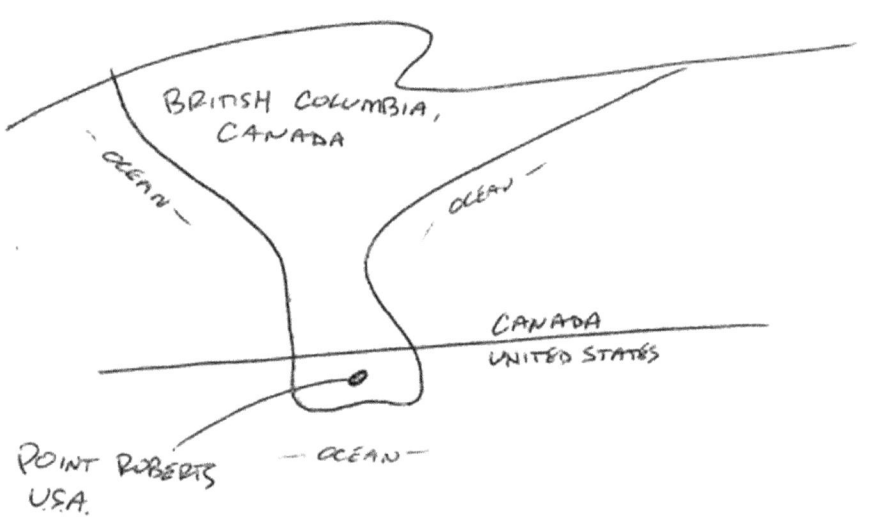

*History:*

In the early 1800s, Spanish, British, American, and Russian soldiers were fighting over the land of Washington State. Eventually, the Americans won the rights, and the Oregon Treaty was signed between British and American politicians to establish the border line between the United Kingdom (Canada) and the USA. Shortly thereafter, the British (Canadians) and the Americans began marking their territory through a survey process. Haphazardly through inaccuracies of the terrain, the southern tip (now known as Point Roberts) ended up under American rule.

This area is shaped like a peninsula that juts out into the Pacific Ocean and is regulated by border patrol agents such that for its own residents to access home turf, they must go through the 4km long Canadian border, or take a boat from "Mainland" USA. Similar to an island, the land is connected to Canada on the north, with the other three sides connecting to ocean, flanking to the east, south, and west.

The industry on Point Roberts is largely based on tourism and the transactions of real estate transactions. One of the landowners in the area is proposing that the US sell the land to Canada, making the entire portion under Canadian Rule.

*Here's the rub, and why geography matters:*
In Point Roberts, American real estate prices are significantly lower than Canadian prices. We're talking big time, $100–300,000 for homes on the American side and one million or more on the Canadian side. These homes are effectively the same bricks and sticks, just divided by the imaginary border line.

**What's #TheHighestAndBestUse?**

The highest and best use of an area with no industry other than tourism and real estate activity would be to accept the policy change, permit Canada to own Point Roberts, and allow the Vancouver market to gentrify this spit of land overnight. If this happened, huge investment activity would open up. According to the YouTube documentary called, "This US City Could Be Sold to Canada," by producer "Off the Cuff," many of the Americans are against the land merger strictly based on merit and generally feel it's disrespectful to those who have resided there for many years.

Cite 9.5

### *1.24d Cloud Seeding*

Even more extreme than #TheHighestAndBestUse of the land is the sky above it. Cloud seeding is a chemical process where scientists propel rockets into the sky, of which artificially impregnate clouds with substances such as silver iodide, potassium iodide, and dry ice. The goal with this activity is to induce the condensation process, which then furthers into snow (cooler climates) or rain (warmer climates).

In the United Arab Emirates, a climate largely based on desert sands and arid extremes, cloud seeding is used to artificially create precipitation in effort to reduce drought. In the US and Canada, it has been used to create snow for ski resorts.

One of the more noteworthy efforts of cloud seeding was the 2008 Beijing Olympics, where athletes had trouble breathing due to smog and heavy manufacturing. Scientists used cloud seeding technology to create city wide artificial rain; this proactively cleared the smog and ensured blue skies prior to the games.

In circumstances such as cloud seeding around a ski resort or a desert, #TheHighestAndBestUse of this land could significantly change with the climate.

Cite 11.5

### *1.24e Steve Wynn's Water Rights at the DI*

Steve Wynn, one of the world's most notorious land developers and hotel casino operators has a brilliant mind when it comes to #TheHighestAndBestUse. Back in August of 2,000, Wynn purchased the property located at 3145 Las Vegas Boulevard South, also known as the "Desert Inn Hotel and Casino" from Starwood Hotels and Resorts Inc. for 270 million USD.

The DI was a luxury destination constructed in the 1950s for travelers and locals seeking entertainment and a trendy atmosphere. Over the years, three hotel towers were constructed for guests, alongside several estate homes, and the early beginnings of a golf course in 1952.

From the developer perspective, there were several key features that this property had built in. Most notably: The underutilized parcel was already located on the Las Vegas strip with existing precedence—the parcel has multiple road frontages with highly marketable traffic, there was thirty-two acres of vacant land included in the sale, and the previously existing golf course was known worldwide. However, there was one feature that Wynn noticed that (possibly) trumped them all was Water Rights.

The soon to be "Wynn Golf Club" came with historic water rights for the groundwater beneath the acreage. With arguably the most lush green grass on the strip, alongside a reported 4,600 linear feet of marsh and wetland, one can imagine how valuable this became.

In 2016, Wynn Resorts proposed a thirty-eight acre blue-water lagoon with white sand beach and additional hotel rooms, something of which no other hotel on the strip could offer. With evaporation rates excruciatingly high in the Nevada Desert, a body of water to this magnitude may only be substantiated with the rights to a consistently producing aquifer.

From a CNBC News article in 2016, Wynn said, "Paradise Park is…taking advantage of imagination and fantasy on property that we own for zero (dollars), with water rights that we own for zero—and we're the only ones that have them at this size."

Cite 12

# #TheHighestAndBestUse
## Golden Nuggets of "Land"

*Chapter 1.00 : #TheHighestAndBestUse of the "Land"*

*Chapter 2.00*

# #THEHIGHESTANDBESTUSE OF THE "STRUCTURE"

## INTRODUCTION

*"You can use an eraser on the drafting table or a sledgehammer on the construction site."*

**~ Frank Lloyd Wright, Architect**

This section on #TheHighestAndBestUse of the "Structure" will have a fundamental look at economic feasibility and construction surrounding residential property. I will talk about some general principles to follow, and how those principles mesh with existing and newly built homes. In order to streamline the examples, I will leave out emotional motivation, investor subculture, and personal influences to keep things concise and objective.

When talking about #TheHighestAndBestUse of a structure, there are four quick questions that I ask myself in order to get a ballpark answer on how to proceed.

1. Income potential "as-is" vs. renovated
2. Cost of construction
3. Time requirement
4. Exit strategy (keep or sell)

If we know these four things, we can make some accurate predictions on how the property may function in its ability to generate maximum income or allow the investor to reach their goals.

## 2.01 THE ART OF MARKET COMPARABLES

*"First we must look at the overall use of the structure…"*

When approaching #TheHighestAndBestUse of a structure that appears to be salvageable, we need to evaluate what that house might be worth repaired vs. how much money it will take to get it there. A common misconception in the industry is that a $100,000 house that gets $20,000 worth of renovations will be worth

$120,000 when it's complete. This is not always true. Certain renovations don't make any money and are considered end user luxuries, and certain renovations return more money than you put in. The net positive difference between money spent vs. completed house value is called "lift" and that is exactly what you're looking for.

First we must look at the overall use of the structure, and for this example we will ask ourselves the big question: Do we reno a lot? Do we reno a little? Do we not reno at all?

Some renovation options here may include:

1. Lightly renovated home
2. Luxury renovated home
3. Un-renovated home
4. Does the home have an opportunity for an accessory apartment(s)/what type?
5. Addition at the rear/side/top

### *Step 1: Gathering Market Comparables*

To determine economic feasibility, you'll need to get market comparables. "Comps," as they are traditionally called, typically come from online sources or real estate professionals. In Ontario, websites like www.housesigma.com give free market comps and allow you to look up properties on your own time, provided they were sold on the MLS. Other paid services such as GeoWarehouse or Purview will give similar information on varying levels of detail.

GeoWarehouse has several features that allow you to look at title transfer history, current owner detail, lot size, lot boundary, legal description, and the price a current/previous owner had paid. The best part about GeoWarehouse is that if a property sells privately (and not on the MLS), the transaction will show up here. Purview is a great tool for appraisers and mortgage brokers to estimate the value of a property based on statistical algorithms, as well as check title, liens, and general property information. Both of these services are a provided for a monthly fee (of which I am unaffiliated).

*Items That Affect Valuations:*

- Maintenance and Repair
- Surrounding Neighbourhood Characteristics
- Lot Size
- House Size
- Gas Station Proximity (land contamination)
- Train Tracks
- Parks and Schools
- End Unit vs. Interior Unit
- Corner Lot vs. Interior Lot
- Proximity to Hospitals and Shopping
- Previous Title Infraction/Transactional History
- Street Name
- Zoning and Future Uses
- Negative Media Exposure
- Drug Use/Grow Op/Gang Activity
- Natural Features Like Trees, Creeks, Waterfront, Views
- Municipal vs. Private Servicing (Well/Septic)
- Outbuildings and Storage
- Current Owner's Motivation to Sell

As for getting direct real estate agent comps, working with a quality agent is a huge asset. I have found that for best results, supporting the same agent over, and over, and over has been of benefit to my business. In similar fashion to a "big fish in a small pond," if you're a major component to an agent's business, they will take your calls, send you more deals, and provide generally better service than a one-off smash n' grab. Remember, the relationship is the most important thing. Relationship value is often worth more than transactional value in a long-standing business. You get what you pay for with quality service providers, and if they can't manage their own money, they probably can't manage yours either.

### Step 2: Building Beneficial Relationships

Asking your agent for comps is a fantastic way to get up-to-date information along with some firsthand industry knowledge. Real estate websites that give data are great but they don't come with that deep market "gut feel" that a seasoned pro inherently possesses.

A few things to keep in mind when asking for comps are:

- How am I supporting this agent's business?
- Is there a future here?
- Am I calling in a favour?

If you're supporting this person's businesses by giving them transactions on the buy or sell side, it's a symbiotic relationship. They give you comps, so you can find deals, and then at some point in the cycle they sell something for you to square the relationship back up. This is good. Asking yourself if there is a future with this person is also good. We talked about relationship value earlier on, this comes into play here.

For example, if you're flipping condos, and your agent is a commercial broker in another city, you may get the market data you need but it (potentially) doesn't come with great relationship value. That agent won't know the specifics of your area and probably isn't in the social and political networks you may need to call on one day.

Also, calling in a favour is fine, but only for so long. Have you ever been asked to move your buddy's house on a long weekend because you're the only guy with a pickup truck? At some point, one side of the relationship feels used, and if you continually ask your agent for comps there is a good chance that person will drop you as a "client" or stop returning your calls. Be fair, pay everyone for their time, or reciprocate.

### Step 3: What to Do When There Aren't Any Comps

If getting directly relatable market comps is challenging in your area due to lack of recent sales, you could also consider costing out the average resale price per square foot of other homes in a wider geographic sample on similar land sizes.

Another method would be to take the average resale price point of the area within a much longer time horizon (rather than ninety days, perhaps use 500 days), and add back the average market inflation or deflation to arrive at an estimate.

Lastly, you could also try to compare your property with replacement cost (new construction). Direct replacement cost is more of an insurance claim type of valuation method because new construction is often more expensive than the existing home's value but it's a start in the right direction. Don't forget to add land value back into the mix.

## 2.02 Vanity vs. Value Markets

*"Home builders are the last to invest in a market, and the first to leave."*

**Loosely tying into valuations from the previous chapter, a "vanity" and "value"** market are two definitions that investors use when deciphering a geographic area for investment.

*Vanity Markets*
Vanity markets are trophy markets and are typically neighbourhoods/cities with high demand that wealthy people want to live in. These markets represent the dream, the luxury, the money, etc. Vanity markets are areas that people go to spend money but not necessarily to work. In other words, this money is coming inbound but not generated there. In vanity markets, it's all service-based industries that serve the wealthy. In a down economy, the vanity markets and luxuries often tumble first and fall the furthest.

Vanity market valuations often exceed the actual construction cost of the home because of the overwhelming opulence. There is a significant up charge for quality design and a fancy postal code. Examples here would be Beverly Hills 90210, Park Avenue Manhattan, Bridal Path Toronto, "The Hamptons," etc.

As a general rule, home builders are the last to invest in a market and the first to leave. This is because there needs to be substantial demand in order to justify the cost of new construction.

*Value Markets*
Value markets always have intrinsic value and are often situated in outlying communities to that of a vanity market. People work in these markets, they live in these markets, and they are not overly flashy. These markets have base utility value and are oftentimes worth less than the construction cost of the home if it were to be replaced. These are the rental markets where people rent instead of buy, and the investor cash flow is more favourable. Again, when it's cheaper to buy the house than to build it, it's often identified as a value market.

*Unique Circumstances*

- Toronto, Canada has so much money floating through the city that it has become a vanity market in price point, while at the same time ensuring the fundamentals of a value market (like jobs) remain in position. It's a vanity market, but it has a huge central business community surrounding it. Some of its features are water access, airports, stock exchanges, train stations, international draw for immigration, fashion, healthcare, music/film, etc. Always look at the fundamental industries surrounding a location before investing or shying away.

- Alberta as a province is largely dependent on the price of oil. When oil is up, everyone moves in, and when oil is down, everyone leaves. So much is dependent on the industry in this location that it could be a vanity market today and a value market tomorrow.

- *"Some areas will never get better, and some areas have already gotten better."* When seeking value markets, #TheHighestAndBestUse is to buy in the transition zone. If you follow the artist community, you will see the next up and coming area present itself. Artists typically move into a location because it's economical (the quintessential "starving artist"), and they bring with them a layer of culture and vibrancy that bleeds into the streets.

- Over time, the middle class see this as the next trendy place to live and they gobble up the real estate because it's mid-range affordable (for now) and not a total dump anymore. With popularity comes appreciation, with appreciation comes higher rents, and with higher rents it forces the art community to go somewhere else (starving artist, remember?). The cycle begins again. Always follow the money, and if you can't follow the money, follow the artists.

## 2.03 Getting Quotes/Working With Contractors:

*"Just because a contractor is in business-for-self, doesn't always mean they are a business person."*

**I want to keep this one short and sweet. I find people over complicate the process** of finding skilled trades. Trades people are generally in more demand than supply, especially the good ones, and this predominantly stems back to the removal of these skilled trades from formal education in the past twenty to thirty years due to liability, cost, and insurance regulation.

Policy makers have missed the boat in realizing that not everything can be done with a computer, and not everything can be outsourced to foreign countries. The problem that has been created from the "top down" is now paid for from the "bottom up." The consumer bears the cost from a labour shortage since supply and demand dictates higher hourly fees from these skilled individuals.

So where do we look for these elusive trades people?

### *Referrals:*
Asking for referrals is the best way to find contractors. Hands down. Presumably if you're asking someone for a referral it's because you trust them, and nobody purposely refers a bad apple. Some avenues to try might be:

Real estate agent
Real estate broker
Friends
Family

Real estate investor (REI) networks
Meet up groups (in person)
Social media posts
Social media REI groups
Experienced investors in your local area

**Cold Searches**

If your referral network has turned up blank, you can then go to the cold search method. Below is a list of places to try first:

Kijiji paid ads and organic ads (note, I prefer crappy unpaid ads)
Craigslist
HomeStars Review service
Google search key terms "contractor near me," "(city) drywall," "best plumbing in (city)
Better Business Bureau recommendations
Social media groups related to construction
Social media groups related to your city
Chamber of Commerce reviews and referrals
Business development online resources from your city

*Here's another one:*
Consider going to the Home Depot/Lowes contractor desks. Ask who's doing what you're looking for. (Who do they see the most? Who's quality? Who's fast? Who's not fast? Etc.).

If they don't have anyone for you, ask for someone in a trade you're not even remotely interested in pursuing. Need a carpenter? Ask for a brick mason. Then call that brick mason and ask for a carpenter referral. The cycle begins again.

**Ok, I've found some people, now what?**
**"The Prelim Project"**

Many new investors fall into the trap of, "Well if I don't have a project to quote, how do I ever know what it's going to cost?" The prelim project is born.

Develop your "ideal situation" that you need help with, perhaps it's a bathroom renovation. You've seen some fixer uppers online through the MLS and notice that most of the bathrooms need similar items. Vanity, tub, tiles, toilet, faucet, paint, and trim. If you're into doing the construction yourself, go spend a day at the big box retail stores pricing out various items. Spreadsheet these items to create a price range, and from there you can create a few averages.

In your spreadsheet, you should have columns for the item, the price, the SKU, and general notes.

For example: | bathroom faucet | $75.99 | #123–456 | chrome two hole.

Do this with myriad items to create the averages, add them up, and voila you have yourself a materials list with stunningly accurate price points.

Next, call your contractors and ask them what your specific bathroom may cost to renovate from the labour perspective (if you're providing materials) or the time and material perspective if you want it done in full. You have now built a material spreadsheet with some general averages for material cost, a rough idea on labour, and learned a ton in the process. This can be scaled from bathrooms to full homes, just start small.

### *Find a Coach*
A construction coach will help you get to where you want to go faster, cheaper, and with more ease than trying to learn it yourself. Mistakes are expensive. Time is expensive. What so many investors forget is that carrying costs add up, connections and networks are time-consuming to attain, industry contacts are invaluable, and nobody can do it alone. There is a reason why Olympic athletes have coaches. It's because they see things in the athlete that the athlete does not see in them self.

> "If you want to make a change, you have to make a change. Education is like a stove, buy it once, use it forever. "

### *Investor Network*
Finding another investor doing what you want can also be hugely beneficial. Perhaps there is an option to drop by their jobsite and see what they're up to. Perhaps when you're at that jobsite you meet that contractor you're looking for, or make an industry connection that sends you down the right path.

### *"Get Three Quotes" Method*

Depending on your market, getting three quotes on something may be tough. In a busy construction season, most contractors are booked months in advance and won't have time to fiddle around while you decide what you want to do, or when you want to do it.

The "get three quotes and pick the one in the middle" method has worked, and will continue to work, but I want to drill down on something more important than price. Price is what you pay, value is what you get.

Imagine a time where you've done ten renovations, and used a different plumber on every job. They will find the time. It comes down to relationships, and the more you support the same people over and over, the more they will have higher regard for you as a top performer and A+ client.

> *#TheHighestAndBestUse Quick Tip: If you find a property that you want quoted in person, pay your contractor to come with you during a viewing. This can be cash, food, gift cards, etc., but make sure its adequate compensation. It's the relationship you want to preserve, and almost nobody does this. Stand out.*

### *Questions to Ask a Potential Contractor:*

Tell me about yourself.
Where are you from?
How long have you been doing this?
What are your specialties?
What are your least favourite jobs?
Have you worked with other investors in the area?

Are you insured?
Do you have workers compensation in event of injury?
Can you provide a copy of this before we start?
What types of problems are you insured for?

What are your billing terms?
How do you invoice, T+M or flat rate?
How do you accept payment?
What are the terms of this payment?

*Other Items to take note of:*
Personal appearance - are they clean?
Are they well-spoken or rude?
What type of vehicle do they drive? Is it maintained?

## *Preferences*

I personally prefer to use a "truck and ladder" crew where possible, dealing directly with the person doing the work. This typically means they have less overhead, and more competitive rates. However, sometimes this can also mean they are over-worked, less reliable, and require more management from you.

On the flip side, a fully polished truck, office staff, storage units, and expensive overhead is baked into the fee somewhere, but it can mean many benefits to the end user such as reliability, less time spent organizing the job, and streamlined planning so you can focus on your highest and best use of what's most important (like doing more deals).

Weigh the pros and cons.

## 2.04 Renovations That Make Money

*"Eye candy will win a dog fight over 'non-pretty' related spending every single time."*

**Kitchen. Bath. Flooring. Paint.**
Kitchen. Bath. Flooring. Paint.
Kitchen. Bath. Flooring. Paint.

Write this down and read it back to yourself.

KBFP is the moneymaker in residential real estate construction. The kitchen and bath is what people appreciate the most, and the flooring and paint is what they see. Eye candy will win a dog fight over "non-pretty" related spending every single time, and pulling permits for that wild idea you had may not pay off. Unless you're going the distance, keep things simple.

There is a clear difference between renovating to flip, renovating for your own enjoyment, and renovating for short-term/long-term maintenance. For the purposes of the below examples, we will use flipping houses as the general direction.

**Kitchen:**

If repurposing the kitchen seems to be in the best interest of the project, this can be done, and typically can be done quite economically.

*Kitchen Cabinets*
- Priming and painting kitchen cupboards is a great way to spruce up the look and modernize a space. If they can be saved, save them. If they've seen their life span, yank it and put in something fresh. Kitchens can run away in price, so do your best to stick with in-stock cabinets vs. getting anything built custom. There are plenty of hardware stores that sell knock-down kits that you can assemble yourself.

*Hardware*
- Trendy hardware/hinges/door pulls will dramatically change the feel of older cabinets. Combine a basic door with a fancy door pull, and it spruces up the kitchen big time. But use a cheapy door with cheapy hardware and it takes you down a notch.

*Countertops*
- Solid surface counters like granite or quartz look beautiful and typically outperform that of laminate. A solid surface will wear better with tenants and also show better for resale, plus allows the under hung sink that so many people prefer. Laminate countertops are ok for certain applications, but before you make that choice, get a quote. By the time you purchase the

laminate, glue the edges, cut the corner angles, seal it, shim it, install it, cut the sink hole, etc., it might have been similar in cost to have a pro come in and seamlessly install something beautiful. Since we're going for maximum lift, weigh the pros and cons here.

*White Appliances vs. Stainless.*
- Both can be considered trendy depending on the environment they are put in. Stainless appliances are attractive on their own, and show well, but dent easily and are difficult to keep clean. White appliances have a tendency to be more economical and easier to find pre-owned. A flat top white stove is common to pick up on Craigslist/Kijiji/newspaper ads for cheap. White is also easier to touch up if it gets scuffed and easier to repair if parts are needed.

*Backsplash*
- The backsplash should be colour coordinated and on point, regardless of rental or flip properties. This is one area that serves function and beauty, and money should be spent here. Choose a nice tile that works with the shape and feel of the room. Subway tile in various forms is a timeless choice, or tiles that make a statement may complement the look you're after. Spend some time and money here.

*Flooring*
- Flooring in the kitchen can be laminate, click vinyl, tile, or hardwood. Whatever you choose, try to use the same flooring throughout the house. One quick tip to make a space feel larger is to remove the transition strips in door thresholds so that all the flooring is seamless and on one level. Spend some time shimming and leveling the floor if needed, it really opens up the space and draws the eye to more important features that you may want to highlight.

*Decor*
- Decor pieces in the kitchen can add that element of warmth and coziness that tenants and buyers will appreciate to make your home feel like theirs. Colour coordinated jugs, potted plants, living green walls, chalkboard paint, or unique dishware will add an element of allure and make the buyers want more. If it's a furnished rental, this is a great way to drive your rents up, and if this is a resale product, consider home staging to get the look you're after.

*Paint*

- Paint should be the same colour as the rest of the house (personal preference). It will blend seamlessly and expand the full building envelope to feel larger. If you have some pro help, colour coordination here will go a long way. Save the paint code to a Google drive folder specific to this project and/or write it inside a cabinet door for future use.

> *#TheHighestAndBestUse Quick Tip: Hire your home stager to pick your finishes for you. Paint, flooring, countertops, trim, etc. They have a knack at design, and they will also know what works best with their furniture once the project gets listed for sale. Start with the end in mind, and work your way backwards. A spreadsheet with product SKUs (as discussed already) goes a long way, and will help you repeat the process multiple times for a one-time consultation fee.*

**Bathroom:**

*Tub vs. Shower*

- For properties with one bathroom, always go with a tub/shower combo. Although a beautiful glass walk-in shower shows well, the tub will be missed by tenants or buyers looking to bathe children or wash their puppy.

*Tile vs. Tub Surround*

- Tub surrounds are relatively inexpensive and they install fairly quickly. Plastic walls and molded corners are leak resistant if installed correctly, and rely on glue or caulking to hold everything together. This is a quick way to cover older style tile or tile board (also known as barker board), and gives a clean appearance. On the other hand, tile is much more durable, and if installed correctly over concrete board or membrane systems, they will be leak proof and last for years. The grout needs to be sealed every so often to avoid discoloration or water seepage but, otherwise, it's an excellent choice. Tile is also very trendy depending on the style you choose and sets the tone for the entire bathroom. The cost for the tile is worth the money spent.

*Flooring*

- There are a few options here, namely tile, click vinyl, or sheet vinyl. Just like a tub enclosure, tile floors are the industry standard and create emotion within the space in a very positive light. They are waterproof, durable, and if the subfloor is stiff enough to accommodate, this would be a great place to use a luxury product. On the flip side, floating floors such as click vinyl or sheet vinyl are great options where you need to quickly cover an old floor up with little mess or effort, or you have a floor that isn't stiff enough to accept solid products. Century homes are notorious for sloping or saggy floor joists, so for an application like this, vinyl may be the best solution. Vinyl products are inexpensive and are installed very quickly. They also can be cut with a knife and installed with minimal experience.

> *#TheHighestAndBestUse Quick Tip: Shy away from any glue down or adhesive backed vinyl flooring. The adhesives can be very difficult to remove down the road, and if they get wet, they may not stick like you had hoped. The glue seams also attract dust, and dust may cause the flooring to lift.*

*Fit/Finish*

- Chrome vs. Brushed Nickel, Black vs. Brass: All of these choices can be made with your hardware as you personally see fit. Trends come in and out every year. Hire someone who knows what's in or get on Pinterest for some clever ideas. Whether it's a farmhouse, country chic, ultra-modern, or bare bones DIY, there are so many options to choose from.

*Trim Details*

- Crown molding or wainscoting panels make for a beautiful bathroom. It's a little added feature like this that sets your four walls apart from your competitions. Crown molding in an average bathroom should cost less than $200 in materials and take no more than a couple hours to install. Preformed wainscoting is expensive to purchase, so in its place you can use several styles of in-stock MDF trim to build a quick faux panel on top of the drywall. Paint the upper half of the room wall colour and paint the lower wainscoting area white. The two-tone look really pops.

*Vanities*

- Vanity purchases can get very expensive, very quickly. If you're in the 24–36" vanity range, they can be purchased off the shelf at most hardware stores. If you're above 36" or are looking for double sink basins/granite tops/custom drawers, you will pay big bucks. Shop around and colour coordinate. Paint the vanity if you need to or swap out the hardware to something that matches the rest of the home. Custom touches on off the rack items make a world of difference at reduced costs.

*Toilet*

- Choosing a toilet is half form, half function. It needs to fit the room, and also fit the toilet flange. Sometimes toilet flanges will be set too close to the wall, and a reduced size toilet tank will be needed. Measure your toilet flange before buying something. Also, if needed, a plumber can install an "Offset Flange," which moves the toilet pipe away from the wall a few inches without major construction.

*General Plumbing and Electrical*

- Spend some money on nice fixtures. For most bathrooms, there are only one or two fixtures to contend with. This sets the tone for the space. Hardware stores, Wayfair, and Amazon all have great fixture choices. Match the colour to your faucets and shower hardware (silver faucet/silver light fixture). Light fixtures are relatively inexpensive for the look and feel they provide. A cheesy DIY bathroom might be a couple hundred bucks in fixtures, whereas a luxury bathroom of the same footprint might only be double that. The little bit extra you spend will pay off. It's not what you spend, it's what you get back on resale.

**Paint**

*Quality*

- Pick a quality paint from a quality manufacturer. Cheap paint is trash, and will take you three coats to cover what could have been done in one. Labour is more expensive than product, and time is the most valuable commodity of all.

*Primer*

- Primer can be tinted if you need to help with coverage and reduce paint coats. For example, if a wall is painted red, it will need several coats to cover and make it uniform. Have the paint store drop a bit of red in the primer base, and it will help reduce your paint coats required. Consider Kilz (water-based) or oil-based primers to block mildew stains and/or smoke smell.

*Interior/Exterior*

- Interior and exterior paint should be used in all spaces. As a general rule, exterior paint is a bit tougher than interior paint, and it also has better wear characteristics for temperature fluctuations in spaces like unheated garages or sheds. Interior paint will peel if the heat gets turned off for an unpaid utility bill. Kitchen/bath paint has mold inhibitors built into the formula to help with spores and moisture issues. Lastly, flat sheen products often cost less than gloss-based products. If you're painting 100 units per year, saving here and there really adds up. Bottom line, Spend the extra 20% and get a decent paint. Save the colour chip so you can touch up down the road.

## 2.05 Renovations That Don't Make Money

*"This is another dollar-for-dollar upgrade…"*

**There are a plethora of renovations in residential construction that don't make** any money. Like, a lot! Certain renovations like the ones discussed in the previous chapter make money because the pretty stuff is what sells. Plain and simple. What's unusually interesting is that even though a nice bathroom gets a potential buyer excited, the redone roof is what really matters. But I digress, here is a list of dead money items that you should avoid if the proposed renovation is about growing the bottom line. For these examples, I'm talking generally about labour and materials. If you DIY everything, and you don't factor in your time as an expense, things may change.

*Windows*
- Windows are expensive to buy, expensive to install, and add little value to a property. Old wood windows are typically single pane and drafty, they need maintenance, they fog up, crack easy, all that. That's crummy. But outfitting an entire house with new windows is a dollar-for-dollar upgrade, and the utility savings (which most people and governments like to gawk about) would take years, and years, and years to realize.

*Roof*
- Re-shingling roofs are a dollar-for-dollar upgrade. There is an expectation of the buyer to just understand the existing roof is decent, and that's that. Whether the roof is two years old or twelve years old, it holds the same monetary value as a function of the building. The exception to the rule is if the roof shingles are fully curled and at the end of their lifespan, then it's money well spent. Tin roofs cost two to three times that of a shingled roof, and unless you have a clear reason for it (forested property, for example), avoid that route.

*Doors*
- Same as windows. Although these do add a function to the property if you are replacing narrow doors for furniture, or the new look of a new front door will enhance the curb appeal, they should generally be avoided for any other reason. Money is made on the land and on the design of a house, not on the construction. We will talk more about this later.

*Driveways and Curb Appeal*
- I say this one gently because there is a lot of moving parts. Basic exterior maintenance, some plants, and a modest driveway will increase the value of a home. Curb appeal wins every time. However, be sparing. Some people like to overspend on their first-time-home-buyer bungalow with stamped concrete facades, waterfalls, and stone landscaping. This will be money that doesn't come back. Side note, if you have a mini mansion and your buyer demands this type of work in your market, different story. Do the work, build it into the price.

*Plumbing Upgrades*
- This is another dollar-for-dollar upgrade. Old, galvanized pipe removal? Cast iron plumbing stack? It's the same as a roof scenario. The buyer "expects" those things to be functioning which gives little upside for you, but a heavy downside on purchase price if they aren't done.

*Electrical Upgrades*
- Removing knob and tube wiring, upgraded electrical panels, all come at a cost. Knob and tube generally means busting holes throughout the house and stringing new wires, only to patch everything back up again as it once was. This means dollars, bro. By the time you spend however much it's going to take, the buyer won't care how long/how much it took to get it there, and again will have just expected this to also be done. However, the insurance company is appreciative.

*Basement Renovations*
- A finished basement for living space is a dollar-for-dollar upgrade. Storage rooms, living rooms, and home offices offer very little lift in value compared to the dollars spent to get it there. If this basement turns into an income producing asset like a basement apartment, or you're able to add beds/baths in a market that demands this, it's a different story.

*Basement Waterproofing*
- This is ungodly expensive and offers little value to the average homeowner. Unless you are putting in a basement suite, a waterproofed basement is similar in nature to a finished basement. Houses shouldn't leak, and if they do, you will get chopped on the price. If they don't, people expect it to be as such, and they carry on. This is a dollar-for-dollar upgrade here as well when we consider the landscaping, driveway, gardens, pools, or AC units that need to be redone outside to complete this task. Interior waterproofing is more economical, especially if the basement is unfinished.

*Detached Garages*
- This one is a 50/50. A really badass detached garage might drive value to certain buyers looking to spend time in the man cave. However, by the time you put up a decent two-car garage that is heated and insulated, you've basically built yourself a second house. It's pricey. Consider: permits, excavation, removal of fill, carrying cost/financing, concrete, foundation, structure, roofing, insulation, wiring, trenching for hydro, hydro panel, drywall, mud, paint, light fixtures, exterior brick or siding, garage doors, windows, etc. Not to mention all the grading and yard work to be done after the fact.

---

**#TheHighestAndBestUse Quick Tip:**

*For these renovations that don't make any yield over and above dollars spent, and you still don't believe me, consider this. If you're buying a used car and the seller tells you the brakes were done two years ago, do you really care? No, you just expect them to work. But if the seller tells you "Oh, the car needs brakes," you'd be pulling out the (proverbial) price reduction handbook and reading it line-by-line for a deeply discounted purchase.*

*It's a phenomenon defined by serviceable and non-serviceable function. If a car part is "serviceable," it may continue its life untouched and has intrinsic value that is expected to be as such. Non-serviceable means the part has no value and will be subtracted from the purchase price in some way, shape, or form.*

*No upside, lots of downside. It's the same in real estate.*

*If you decide not to fix something that is in clear disrepair, disclose it to the buyer.*

## 2.06 "Using the Existing Structure" for Renovations and Economic Feasibility Questions to Ask Yourself

*"How much time will this property take to turn around with extensive renovations…?"*

There are several types of structures when it comes to residential investing: Single detached, townhouse/row house, condo building, semidetached, two story or three story, bungalow, split level, multifamily apartment. When you are evaluating the economic feasibility of a project and have the inclination that it makes most sense to keep the existing structure (as opposed to tearing it down), we begin by relating back to previous chapters first.

1. Market comparables
2. Getting contractor quotes
3. Renovations that make money
4. Renovations that lose money

Once we roughly know the answers to these items, we can then determine which direction to take the project. In future chapters, we will discuss the actual skill set of an investor and how they can determine what #TheHighestAndBestUse is for them from a competency perspective. In the meantime, some questions that are worth doubling back on are:

1. Income potential "as-is" vs. renovated
2. Cost of construction
3. Time requirement
4. Exit strategy (keep or sell)

*Income Potential:*

What is the long-term income potential by renovating to a specific built form? One unit? Three units? Ten or more units? If this is a short-term flip, how much can you profit by upgrading the final product? What's it worth as-is?

*Cost of Construction:*
How much will this built form cost to achieve? Will it take more money to upgrade then the market dictates it's worth when complete? Will there be lift" on the property over and above the money spent when complete? Where can the renovation get complicated? What's the upside potential and downside risk?

*Time Requirement:*
How much time will this property take to turn around with extensive renovations? How much time are you available to give this property on a daily/weekly/monthly basis? How does financing affect the speed at which this project must be completed? What happens if it takes more time than anticipated? Are there any upsides in being completed faster?

*Exit Strategy:*
How do you exit this project? Is it a buy and hold investment requiring a refinance of the capital on completion? Do you sell the property on the open market for reclamation of those funds? If it doesn't sell, what happens? If it sells for over/under asking price would you be satisfied? Is there a plan A, B, C?

*Strategies to boost rent:*
What can be done to increase rents to market value or above market value? Do you include extras that other landlords in the market don't offer? Do you include special features to the property that are low cost and high value?

*Finishes:*
What is most likely to receive the best results for time and money spent? Low end cosmetic renovation/upper mid-range finishes for broadest appeal/ultra-luxury meticulous renovation? What does the market demand in this area?

*Appliances:*
Do white used appliances suffice? Do they need to be stainless and brand new? Does your buyer expect top of the line equipment? Are big box retail appliances sufficient in this area or do the appliances need to be imported?

*Amenities:*
Pools, wide driveway, garage, storage, car wash, landscaped areas, etc. Do any of these play a factor in the resale price or refinance value of the property?

## 2.07 "Teardown" Structures, Values, and Process

*"In order to qualify for that new building permit submission, you will need the following items."*

In the new construction residential market, a developer may purchase a piece of property that has an existing residence on it that's at the end of its life expectancy. To determine #TheHighestAndBestUse, we must see the current value of that parcel in a few different ways. If the economic feasibility in the "Using the Existing Structure" chapter has turned out poorly, perhaps that house should be demolished in favour of new construction opportunities. If so, the following information will be of importance. Here's what to look for.

### Land Value - Value vs. Price

Something to consider when tearing down a structure is the cost of demolition on a previously developed building lot vs. raw land value. If you're looking at a piece of land with a $100,000 price tag and are comparing apples to apples, make sure you factor in the cost of demolition, utility servicing, and the upside of a development charge (credit) vs. that of the fully vacant land.

| TEAR DOWN HOUSE | | RAW LAND | |
|---|---|---|---|
| MARKET VALUE | $140K ←SIGNIFICANTLY DIFFERENT→ MARKET VALUE | | $100K |
| UTILITIES | $0 | UTILITIES | $25K |
| DEVELOPMENT CHARGES | $0 | DEVELOPMENT CHARGES | $20K |
| DEMOLITION | $5K | DEMOLITION | $0 |
| BUILD READY | 145K | BUILD READY | $145K |

In the above example, If raw, undeveloped land has a market value of 100k, the local development charge is 20k and utility servicing costs are 25k, the total cost for a build-ready lot if 145k. Conversely, if a tear down house goes for sale, a builder needs to map out all of the costs and credits to come up with market value in reverse before purchasing. As seen, there are 0 development charges (because they were already paid when the existing house was built), the utilities are existing, but the demolition cost to remove the structure is 5k. All net net, that house is theoretically worth 140k on the open market.

As you can see, 100k for raw land and 140k for what "seems" to pretty well be raw land, are both very different numbers. In this example, if the tear down house was sold for 100k, the builder would have got a great deal. And if the raw land sold for 140k, the builder would have likely overpaid Do the math.

Too many times people will try to compare what they think the value of the land is based on other parameters, but at the end of the day, it's not a perceived market comparison method that counts, it's economic feasibility. Some sales agents will often list land and exclude sales tax, servicing, development charges or credits, or other similar items because they aren't developers, and they just don't know.

There are several other costs to consider when contemplating new construction, and this example serves as a thought guide, not the only arithmetic you need.

### *Development Charges*

If the property is to be redeveloped, the house upon the land typically carries what is called a development charge (DC) credit. In some cities, there may be zero development charges attributed to new construction anyways, and in other cities a development charge may be extremely expensive. In short, a DC is a fee that is paid to the government giving you the rights to build on that land. Every government uses DCs differently; some policy makers attribute that fee to the school board, some to municipal servicing or infrastructure development.

It makes little difference to the developer where those fees go, but the fact is that if you have to pay it, it should be a line item in your budget. As a general rule, if you take down a single-family home, you will get one DC credit equaling the value of one single-family home. You are effectively swapping like-for-like and can continue on with the build without incurring any additional expense here.

## Demolition Permit

A demolition permit is explicitly what it sounds like—a permission from the governing body to remove a structure from the subject lands. This may include a garage, a permitted deck, a cold cellar, a detached outbuilding, or the entire home itself. Typically when a demolition permit is issued, there is a set timeframe at which the demolition must take place in order to maintain public safety or push a public agenda for gentrification.

Prior to demolition, all city services must be disconnected and signed off. These services typically include:

- Hydro
- Natural gas
- Telephone
- Internet
- Fiber optics
- Sewer lines
- Storm drainage
- Water pipes
- And any other underground/overhead infrastructure critical to the operation of the land.

Private services, such as well heads, septic beds, and underground oil tanks are also a consideration as they may pose a hazard to the environment and future construction. There may be disconnection fees associated with removing a utility from a parcel of land—this is something that is important to confirm with the utility company prior to removing conditions on a purchase.

## Utility Locates

"Locates" as they are typically called, are a series of drawings provided by the governing body to find any underground infrastructure that may affect your demolition/development proposal. These are generally requested weeks in advance and are critical in moving the project forward. As a general rule, the contractor or homeowner doing the work is to call in their own locates, and any outsourced contractors would need to confirm the locates are valid before commencing construction activity. Work requiring locates would include the demolition of a home, but also fence/deck installs, septic system excavation, sprinkler pipe or irrigation networks, trenching, deep driveway excavation, retaining walls, etc.

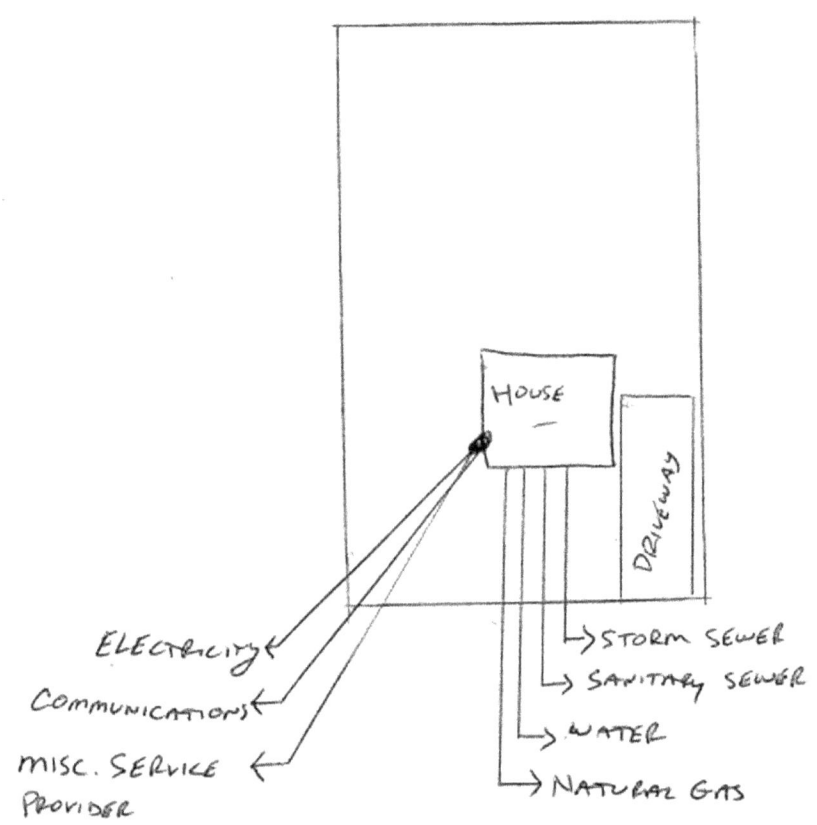

> **#TheHighestAndBestUse Quick Story: A True Story on Utility Connections**
>
> *On a recent project that I was constructing, the demolition had taken place and a new structure was being built. I approached the governing electrical authority to bring hydro back into the property as the overhead service line was previously disconnected. The hydro company replied and said that I had to bring the hydro from the existing pole, underground, down the boulevard, across the street, and up to this home at a cost of $46,000. This was insane and not in the budget.*
>
> *According to them, there was a city bylaw that mandated underground services to be the new normal. I asked to see the bylaw, to which it could not be provided. After speaking with several city councilors and other officials, it was determined that somebody had made a "judgment call" and just thought that an underground service simply looked better. I pushed to have the overhead service reinstalled, as it matched the character of the neighbourhood. It was installed for under $1,000.*

### *New Construction Submissions For Building Permits*

As we discussed back in the chapter on #TheHighestAndBestUse of the land, the zoning will generally dictate what can be built on the parcel. If the general consensus and pre-consultation tells you that it's a single family home, then it's a single family home. If there is an opportunity for more density, and that has been evaluated with economic feasibility, move forward. Your site plan will have dictated the structure's footprint, and now it's time to submit the building's floor plans for review.

In order to qualify for that new building permit submission, you will need the following items:

1. Site plan
2. Grading plan and topographic survey
3. Elevations and floor plans of the building to be constructed
4. Servicing plan

5. Heating Ventilation Air Condition (HVAC) calculations
6. Licensed tradesperson registration numbers as required by your jurisdiction
7. Finances to pay for the application and permit fees
8. Engineering paperwork for roof truss and floor joist systems
9. Engineering paperwork for other building code requirements
10. Site specific information requested by building official

## 2.08 Additional Residential Dwelling Units - The Basement Apartment

### The "Gold Standard" Basement Apartment

**The gold standard of two-unit conversion would undoubtedly be the** "basement apartment." Because there has been heavy emphasis on basement apartments over the years and the industry wide available information is endless, we won't spend too much time here but it should be touched on for general knowledge sake.

The basement apartment by definition is the most economical way to add density and income generation to a property. Because cities are looking for higher densities within urban areas, and also on existing infrastructure, the basement suite is a great way to take underutilized square footage and create living units that are clean, safe, and affordable.

As a general rule, one of the most expensive activities you can do with construction is to add new square footage. A basement (whether finished or otherwise) is something that is built into a house's structure *"by default."* Yes, there are slab-on-grade houses in many cities, but even those houses need a foundation dug, and geo-technical constraints aside, it makes more sense to pour foundation walls for full basements for utility purposes than to backfill that excavated area with stone.

To further illustrate my point of *"by default"* construction, consider an attic space with high ceilings of similar nature to that of an empty basement, that can be further utilized for interior living accommodations. The structure is built and already exists *"by default"* on day one of house completion, it's simply misused for what it could be. Basements for income properties are the same.

In an existing single family home, all of the services needed to use that house *(by default)* already exist—furnace, hot water tank, municipal servicing, hydro panel and connections, the roof, the foundation, etc. If the house didn't have these, it wouldn't be a house. In true #TheHighestAndBestUse fashion, these existing features are under-utilized and can support a better use of the structure.

Developing basement apartments are very similar to developing land. It requires zoning, permits, site plan for parking, etc. The main difference being that there is significant leniency when it comes to "adding to existing" vs. "creating new," and since you aren't changing the fabric of the neighbourhood by popping an extra unit down below, many cities appreciate the intensification.

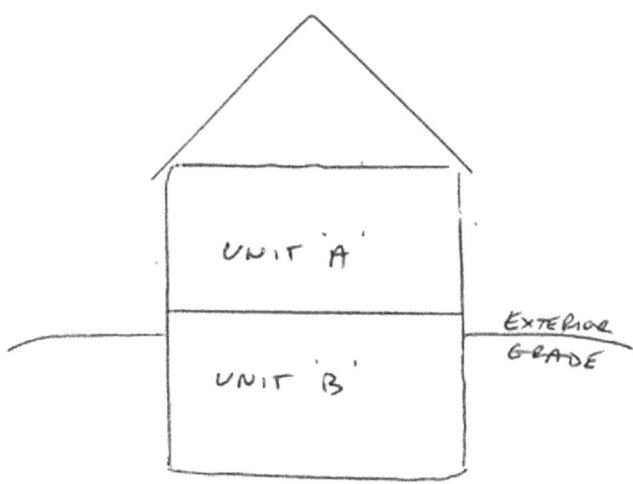

## 2.09 Additional Residential Dwelling Units - The Vertical Split

*"I coined a term called 'The Vertical Split'…"*

**In my early days of investing when legal two-unit conversions were at the coming**-of-age phase, I coined a term called, "the vertical split." The vertical split was a renovation technique that I created to change the way that two-unit conversions on existing residential properties were being done.

Using a bungalow for this example, the majority of the industry was taking existing homes, renovating the main floor, and adding a basement apartment in the bottom level. Two units were achieved and both would list on the open market for fair market rent.

The limiting factor I saw in this model is that the main floor unit would always rent for more money than the basement unit because the main floor had more natural light and was often slightly larger. This represented an opportunity and a challenge. How do we get the basement unit rent higher, without affecting the moneymaker on the main floor?

Utilizing the same building code and zoning techniques that were already in use for two-unit conversions, I proceeded to design a model that had walls separating the units vertically, so both units had main floor <u>and</u> basement access. A second set of stairs was installed for these purposes which then gave both units the "feel" of a townhouse and equal natural light, all within the existing permitted zone. The homes would on average rent for 10–20% more than the traditional "basement apartment" model, and the tenants had a better quality of living.

As you can see here in the layouts below, there are several examples of how I was cutting up existing properties in bungalows, split-level homes, two-story homes, and further. The technique has since been adopted into the majority of my new construction business to this day. In two-unit conversions, I often consider this to be #TheHighestAndBestUse.

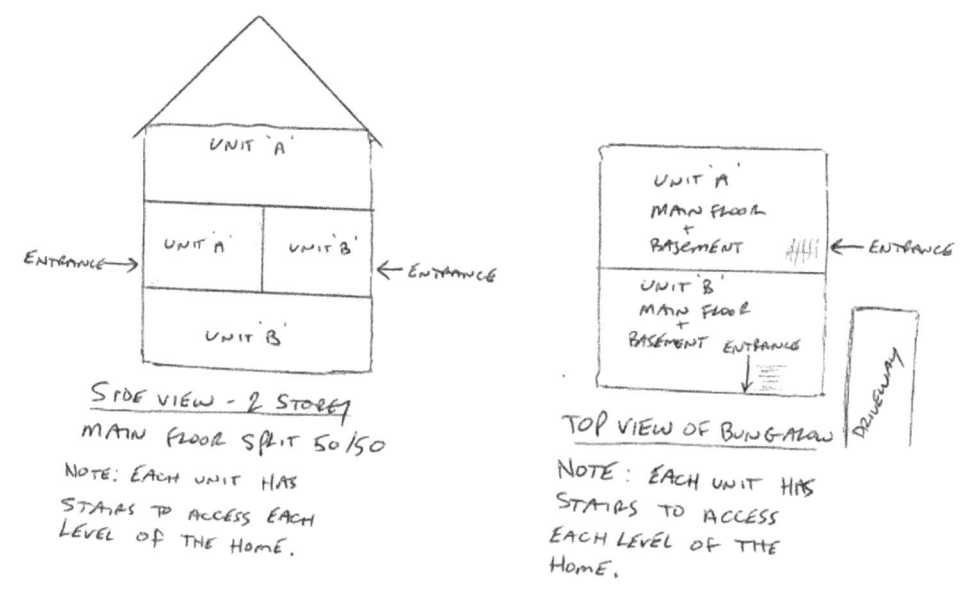

## 2.10 Additional Residential Dwelling Units - Dwelling Units Within Accessory Buildings

*"I use the term coach house because I feel it's the most eloquent way to represent..."*

**In Ontario, coach houses are the new basement apartment.** Years ago, the basement suite breezed into the market as the new normal. Every house that had the ceiling height for a unit below grade and some parking for an additional car was (and still is) getting a basement apartment. By definition, a "dwelling unit within an accessory building" would simply be a small stand-alone residential house that is intended for living accommodations on an existing parcel of land, where it is secondary in nature to that of the principal dwelling.

Today, the accessory building with a dwelling unit is in its infancy and ripe to grow. It's not the same song as the basement apartment, but it's on the same album, from the same artist, in the same genre.

There are several names for these types of units: Coach house, tiny house, laneway house, accessory building dwelling unit, detached accessory unit, granny flat, etc. Literally dozens and dozens of names. For this, we will use "coach house."

When we evaluate #TheHighestAndBestUse of a site plan, often (but not always) more units equals more rent, more rent means more income, and more income means higher property values. Once we determine that more units do actually correlate to the given circumstance, we must decide on what type of unit is to be added. In the case of multifamily buildings that might mean cutting up a two bedroom into a pair of one bedrooms. In the case of low rise residential, adding units might mean basement apartments, top up renovations, or in this example, a coach house.

I use the term coach house because I feel it's the most eloquent way to represent what these structures are/were in the past. The history of the coach house stems from servants quarters, of the servants who typically looked after farmland or equestrian uses on a large family estate. What's unique about the coach house in this example is that the landowner would reside in the principal dwelling, while the hired help resided in their own dwelling unit separately, and invisible to guests. In modern times, the coach house will be used for additional income, multigenerational living accommodations, or accessible living accommodations where stairs and medical access are a concern. On an infill residential application, certain building characteristics are required to fit the lot boundary in order to best use the structure, make the site function, and provide additional parking if required as per the zoning bylaw.

### *Site Plan*

Every city is different with respect to how they see coach houses or if they promote them at all, and for the purposes of this chapter we will do a site plan based on some generalities using detached garage structures as a starting point

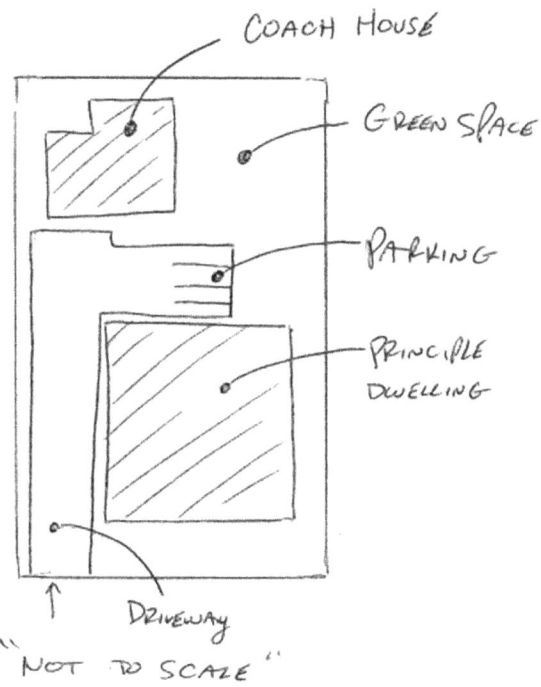

#### #TheHighestAndBestUse Quick Tip:

*It's interesting to note that coach houses have been around for a long time but only recently have they become the topic of discussion in Ontario specifically through a bill titled "Bill 108, More Homes More Choice Act." In 2019, this bill enacted a provincial mandate for further housing intensification within existing urban boundaries.*

## *Servicing*

The servicing of a coach house is extremely important because it is not in any way similar to that of an internal basement apartment. With the internal basement apartments, you would typically have a water main and sanitary sewer coming into the building which would tee off inside the residence to satisfy your servicing in your building permit. With a coach house, because the structure is fully detached and away from the principal dwelling, the services must be run underground to prevent freezing and damage from recreational traffic.

If your home's principal dwelling already has two units within the four walls, and the coach house is the third unit, there's a very good chance you will need to upsize the water main in order to provide adequate supply to all units. Very common in this case is a 1" water service, while typically the existing 4" sewer sanitary pipe is sufficient. Without getting into the weeds on specifics behind water/sewer servicing, for standard residential construction this should be satisfactory. In larger buildings or larger developments, six or more" sewer pipes become the norm with engineering that is outside the scope of this book.

When servicing the coach house, the applicant needs to be prepared for additional costs related to servicing of that structure. These include:

- Ripping up the yard
- Removing pools
- Removing driveways
- Damaging landscaping
- New sod
- Relocation of air conditioning units
- Deck replacement
- Grading alteration
- Fence removal for machinery access
- Curb and roadway deposits

All of these things need to be taken into account because you have to trench from the existing dwelling to the coach house, and in some cases up to 10' below grade. This might be a good time to consider doing some additional work around the site while it's already in a mess, such as exterior waterproofing on the principal dwelling.

### *Construction*

The construction of a coach house from a building perspective is slightly different from that of a detached garage. A detached garage is often built as a slab on grade design where the slab floats with the frost and the footings of the slab only protrude 12–18" below the topsoil. In the case of a residential dwelling, you must have adequate 4' of frost coverage to prevent the house from heaving. If you have an existing detached garage, you will either have to take it down in place of a new foundation or update the existing foundation with frost covered protection. Don't get caught in the trap of saying, "Hey, I could put a living suite in here for a couple thousand bucks and we're good to go." It doesn't work like that. Most of the time, it's best to start fresh.

Depending on your zoning bylaw, the footprint of the building may be the only limiting factor in the size of your coach house, thereby making second stories or basements permissible within those rulings. For example, a 500 ft² coach house footprint might be the equivalent to a 1,000 ft² coach house if you could add a basement, or a 1,500 ft² coach house if you add a basement and second story loft. If there is nothing preventing a basement in a coach house, this is often the most economical way to add more square footage for bedrooms or living space because the basement does not need exterior finishing like a second story does, and a basement already has to be dug for proper footings and foundation anyways. Refer back to the chapter on basement apartments for further information here. You might as well make #TheHighestAndBestUse of that open cavity by filling it in with living space for the tenant "by default."

On the topic of second stories on coach houses, it's very common for a municipality to limit the height of an accessory structure to: Some percentage of the existing dwelling, a measurement compatible with the existing character of the neighbourhood, a ratio of the structure's footprint, or just a flat out number restricting the overall height to a set point on the roof. See below for an example from the Oshawa City zoning bylaw that defines the three ways they measure how large an accessory structure can be.

*The most restrictive of:*

    a. *Eight percent (8%) of the lot area;*

    b. *Fifty percent (50%) of the lot coverage of the main building on the lot; and*

    c. *60m² of ground floor area.*

Although at the time of this writing, coach houses in the traditional sense have not been approved in this city, yet, a good starting point for those rulings would stem from existing policy on accessory structures. If your city is in a similar position, this would be useful information.

### *Exterior Design*

A unique component to coach house design would be the physical shape of the building in order to give tenants privacy. Rectangular buildings are often easy to build, quick to construct, have less hips and valleys in the roof, and are a very simplistic defined space. If we take this one step further and create an L-shape structure, things get interesting.

The unique part about coach houses is such that when building these structures they are often in backyards of existing principal dwellings whereby the privacy can feel restricted if careful design consideration hasn't been tended to. By designing an L-shape cut out to the side yard or rear yard setback, the builder will naturally produce a courtyard atmosphere for tenant amenity space. Things like barbecues, patio furniture, and small gardens are a perfect way to use this space and make the tenant feel as if you care. Because you should, after all it is your investment, and happy tenants pay rent. It's an old saying in raising private capital, that if you go in for money you come out with advice, and if you go in for advice you come out with money.

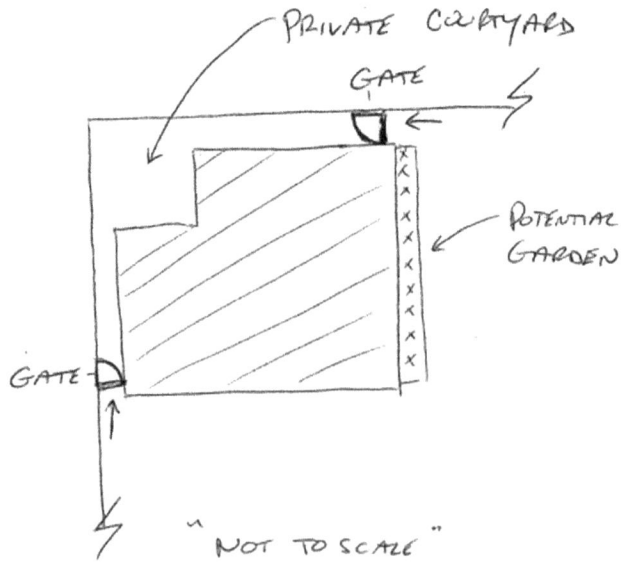

The same principles apply with tenants. If you go in with design in mind, you will come out with a positive result. If you go in looking to maximize the rent and scrimp on the tenant, you will come out with problems. Put the tenant first. The capital expense on the structure is a one-time cost (excluding maintenance) and you will be fortunate to reap benefits for years to come as long as you own that asset. Spend the time.

*Exterior Materials*

From an exterior construction perspective, your options would traditionally be siding or masonry to clad the exterior facade. Depending on what the principal dwelling has on its exterior, you can make the decision to either complement that building by using identical building materials or take the coach house in a different direction so that it is a standalone design. Money is made here in design so adding a beautiful structure will generate more rent because it touches the emotional decision-making side of the brain.

*Exterior Siding*

For exterior siding products, your choices would commonly be vinyl horizontal or vinyl board and batten styles. This product is often the most economical in lighter shade colours because the vinyl can be made thinner and doesn't warp from the sun. It is also more resistant to fading because darker colours hold the heat. Darker colours are available in vinyl siding products but will cost slightly more because they need to be built thicker and more robust. Other types of siding are often made of wood or composite materials with the colour being pre-impregnated into the mould or liquid stained if the material is porous. There are plenty of good exterior grade wood products that can be stained to match the existing structure.

*Exterior Masonry*

Masonry products would include block, brick, natural stone, or veneer stone. It is very common to see a brick structure top to bottom, skirted with a stone product approximately 3' up from the base, with vinyl siding in the gables. Colours, shades, and variations aside, this is done strategically. Oftentimes the more movement, roof peaks, and accentuations you have in the structure, provided they work harmoniously with each other, the more value you add vs. that of flat shaped and single shaded buildings. Brick and stone break up the eye to create character at a lower level, whereas vinyl siding in gables and peaks are commonly used because it is lighter to carry up scaffolding and requires less structural reinforcement over windows openings. Other choices here for gables would be things like cedar shake, which gives a cottage nautical vibe in some cases, and "garden" feel in others.

### *Interior Design*

Interior finishes on a coach house should be decorated to the design standards of your market as per what your market tenant may dictate. I personally prefer upper mid-range finishes in most markets because it is the most versatile and easiest to accomplish vs. that of ultra-luxury. Upper mid-range finishes can appeal to the entry level market, the mid-range market, as well as the luxury market for different reasons.

The entry level product market always likes nice stuff. End of story. However, that market demographic is less exposed to this type of finish as a general rule, which makes a unit of this character financially achievable if the tenant is able to strive for the next rung on the ladder.

The mid-level (median) market just expects mid-level finishes because that's what they have been preconditioned to recognize, so upper mid-range finishes would be the norm here. The median price point in the market is a financial figure that many investors base their decisions off of.

Upper mid-range finishes in the luxury market would be considered a slight downgrade from what that market may be used to, but with that also comes a reduction in price making it slightly more attractive if the luxury market buyer is looking to save a few bucks. All in all, it's just good practice to target upper mid-range finishes, and it doesn't take that much more money to make something beautiful vs. making it look cheap. It's the same amount of labour to install a $9 used door handle from a garage sale, as it is a $29 trendy new one. The end result from a design perspective is of significance.

## 2.11 THE YELLOW HOUSE STORY - WHERE IS THE MONEY MADE?

*"It's not the act of building the house that generates income…"*

**In the developer-builder mindset, money is made in real estate in two ways.** It's made on the land and it's made on the building design—it is not made in construction. Construction is inherently a low margin business and oftentimes just a vehicle to get from point A (raw land) to point B (finished product). To illustrate my point, read on.

Take for example a 2,000 ft², three bed, two bath home that's built in a great neighbourhood. The builder erects this house with all of the traditional building materials and then proceeds to colour coordinate everything in bright yellow. I'm talking about everything in bright yellow—the shingles, the walls, the driveway, the flooring, the toilets—everything bright yellow.

A prospective buyer comes in and says, "Well, this is a brand new house, very interesting, but it's ugly. I'll offer you less than market value."

Now take that same house, same builder, same bricks and sticks. Rather than coordinating everything in bright yellow, a design coordinator comes in to choose colours, finishes, and all visual materials. They select beautiful flooring, architectural shingles, designer fixtures, etc.

That same prospective buyer walks into the structurally identical house and says, "Wow, this house is beautiful. I'll pay you over asking price."

The point I am illustrating here is that it's not the act of building the house that generates income, it's the way that it touches the buyer's emotions. In both examples, the house was considered to be brand new, with the same drywall, the same labour for flooring, the same labour to install a shingle, but the difference here was that the first example was ugly and the second example was stunning. It was the same underlying fundamentals to put all of that structure together.

I go back to my original point—money is made in the land, money is made in the design, it is not specifically made on the construction. We have officially separated the construction activity out of this example and pinpointed where the dollars are created.

## 2.12 Alternative Construction Options For Additional Units and Unique Structural Renovations

*"Breezeways, Bridges, and Tunnels…"*

**Some of the examples that we talk about discuss "doing less" to maximize profit** or increase speed. But sometimes we're leaving opportunities on the table by seeing deals the same way as everybody else. In this section, let's talk about some additional creative ways to find value and increase project viability with structures, built form, and architecture. The educational component is critical to achieving #TheHighestAndBestUse.

*Top Up Renovations:*

Taking a smaller home, removing the existing roofline, and adding a second, third, or fourth story for additional units. Top up renos are common in markets where low rise bungalows are less preferred by buyers, in comparison to two or more story homes.

Sometimes, #TheHighestAndBestUse here is the unlocking hidden potential for a scenic view. Rooftop patios on flat roof designs are also a value add.

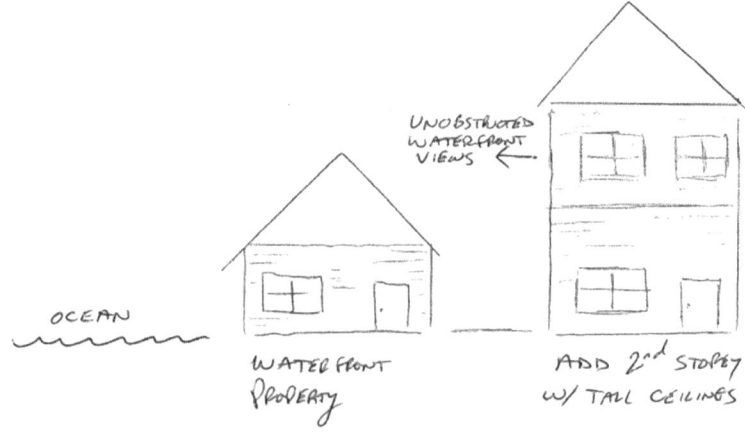

## Full Addition

Adding square footage to the rear or side of an existing structure for the purposes of additional units is a very common request of building departments to add onto the existing structure with new construction, and in doing so may bypass a series of government planning measures that would otherwise apply to a fully new build.

Consider #TheHighestAndBestUse for an addition to include avoidance of items like road widening expropriation, site triangle allowance, and utilizing legal non-conforming setbacks to their fullest potential. In some cases, an addition also permits additional square footage to be added without any charge in government sales tax on the existing asset.

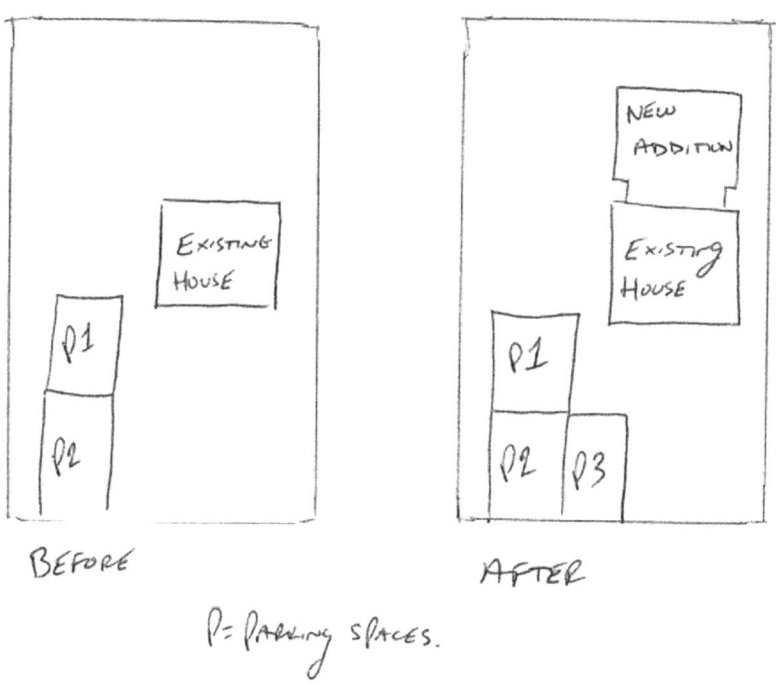

## Underpinning

Using a low basement ceiling height to its fullest potential by "digging out" or lowering the existing concrete slab.

#TheHighestAndBestUse of underpinning is commonly used in highly populated urban centers where houses are connected to their neighbours or when jacking up of a house cannot be achieved. This type of construction is done in phases with new footings being poured sequentially to redistribute the load and prevent settling of the structure.

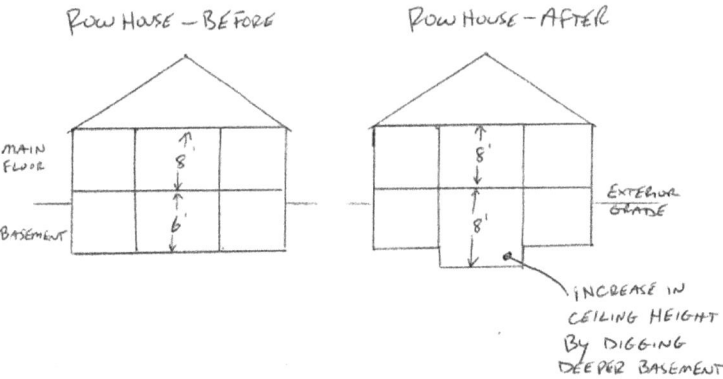

### *Lifting/Jacking Up Structure*

This is the process of raising a house with a low basement in order to gain additional ceiling height or modify the curb appeal.

Consider #TheHighestAndBestUse on a project like this where other houses in the market with specific characteristics cannot be readily attained or where economics may otherwise justify it. Pay attention to the age, structural stability, soil conditions, weather, time, and overall cost to complete. In most cases, a homeowner's belongings can stay in the property during this type of a project as the interior of the finished dwelling can remain unaffected.

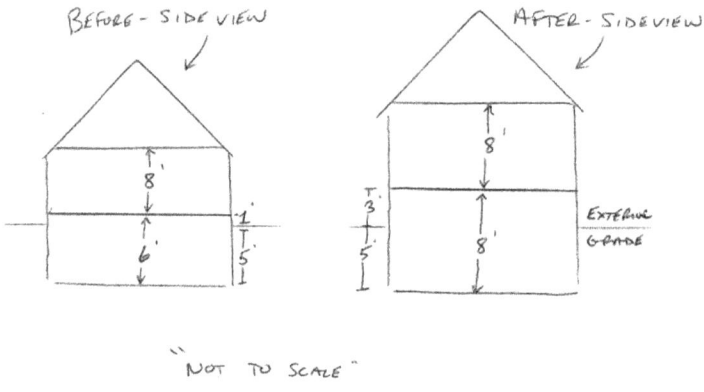

## Moving the Structure

It is common practice to move a completed structure of a house onto a preferential parcel of land (using municipal roadways) or relocating a structure on its own existing parcel.

Consider #TheHighestAndBestUse here to involve the preservation of historical assets where money can't buy a replacement. Also, if a house is attained for $0 (which prevents the existing owner from paying demolition costs), it can be relocated and reinstalled on a new parcel.

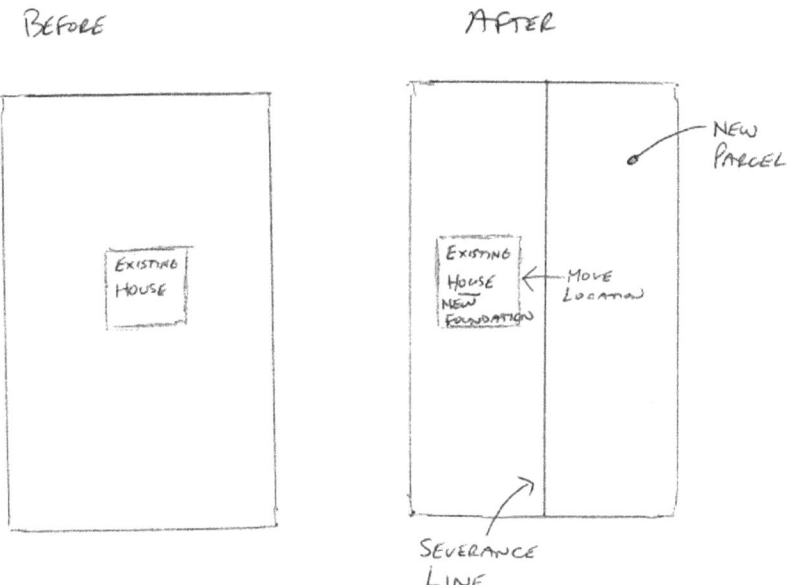

## Structural Cantilevers

In certain situations, houses or buildings that must have a fixed footprint can be built with a foundation as per specification but with a structure that overhangs on one, two, three, or all sides. This effect creates additional interior square footage while still complying with lot coverage/natural drainage/driveway/parking requirements. See Example A..

Example B: Consider #TheHighestAndBestUse of a building with a 25'x25' (624sf) footprint on the main level, and two stories of 32x32 above it (1,024sf per level).

If the builder was limited to 624sf throughout, that's enough for a one bed/one bath unit on the main floor and the same above. With the additional engineering of cantilever floor systems protruding 3.5' on all four sides, that same project would contain the one bed/one bath on the main floor and a whopping three bed/two bath on each of the engineered upper levels. Plug those numbers into your pro forma!

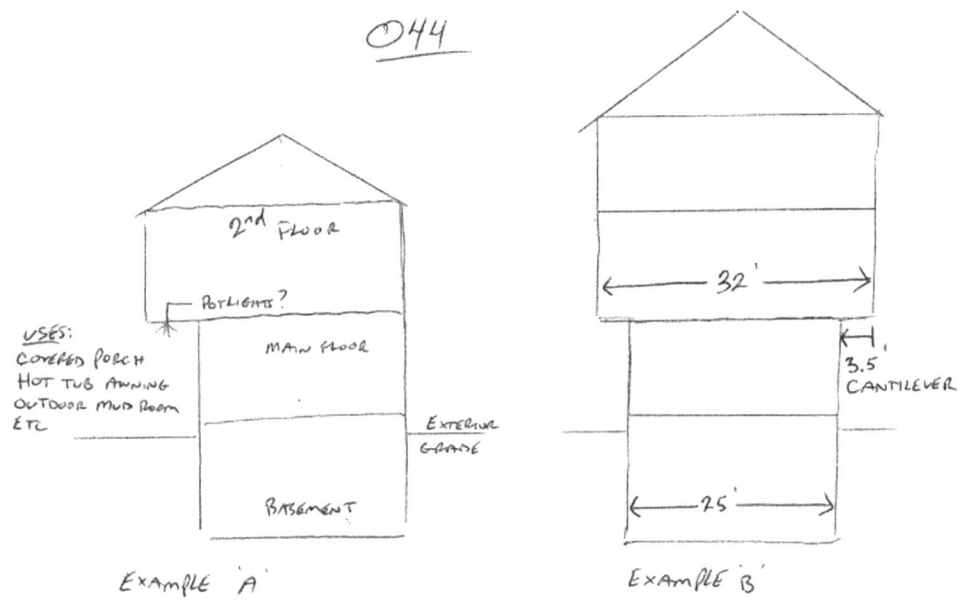

### The Corner Lot Sight Triangle Fix

Corner lot buildings in downtown locations (where land comes at a premium) can fall prey to the dreaded "sight triangle" rulings whereby the building can't protrude into the visible line of sight for oncoming traffic.

To combat this, #TheHighestAndBestUse would be a mult-story building which cantilevers the second or third story above the site triangle area, while maintaining the ground level free of visible encumbrances. If rent is priced on a "per square foot" basis, and thereby the value of the development would follow suit, the cantilevered engineering and structural reinforcement costs are justified.

*Chapter 2.00 : #TheHighestAndBestUse of the "Structure"*

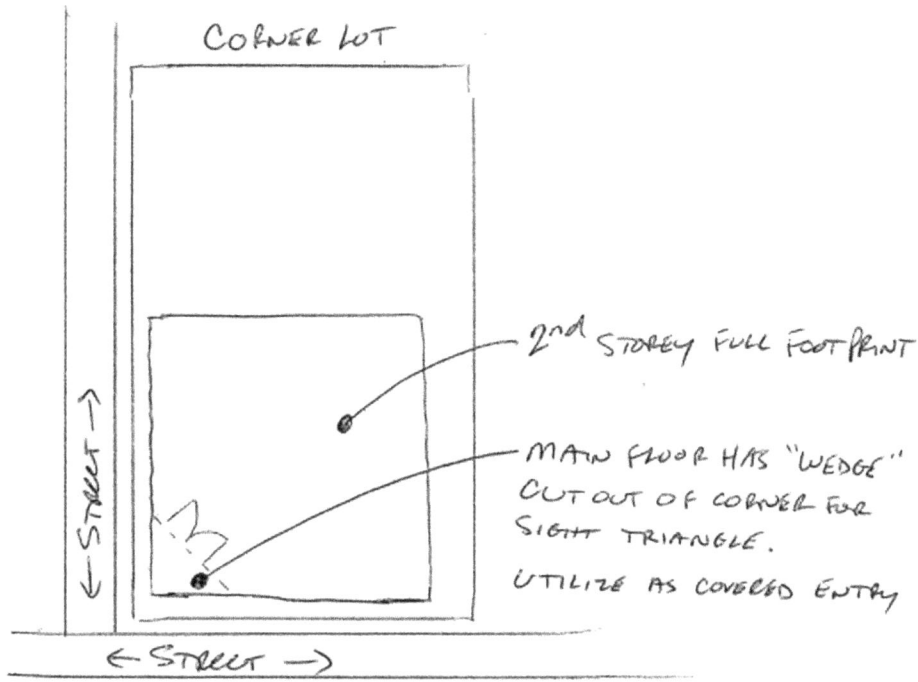

### *Roof Dormers*

In older homes with low ceiling height in second story living areas, or newer homes that want additional natural light for upper floor lofts, accessory units, or office spaces, a roof dormer may be an option here. If a builder is looking to convert an attic to living space and doesn't want to rip the roof off, consider a series of dormers.

These add #TheHighestAndBestUse of curb appeal and give the property significant ceiling height increases. Dormers are very common in century homes, cape cod style homes, bungalows with high roof pitch, and many more models.

If you've seen 20th Century Fox's *Home Alone* where Kevin McCallister (Macaulay Culkin) leaps out the back of his house onto a zip line rope, he does so through the use of a dormer. Faux dormers are also an option to add character to a structure.

### *Breezeways, Bridges, and Tunnels*

Connecting a house to an accessory structure with a breezeway, bridge, or tunnel. Some ZBLs consider a breezeway, bridge, or tunnel to be an addition to the principal dwelling provided it is heated and attached permanently to both the principal dwelling and the accessory structure. Because of this classification, you often need to comply with the zoning regulations for the principal dwelling, not an accessory structure. Typically, accessory structures are restricted for footprint, height, overall use, plumbing, and/or living quarters, however, additions are not restricted in the same manner.

To achieve #TheHighestAndBestUse of a larger garage then the ZBL permits, for the look and feel of a coach house, connect the dots.

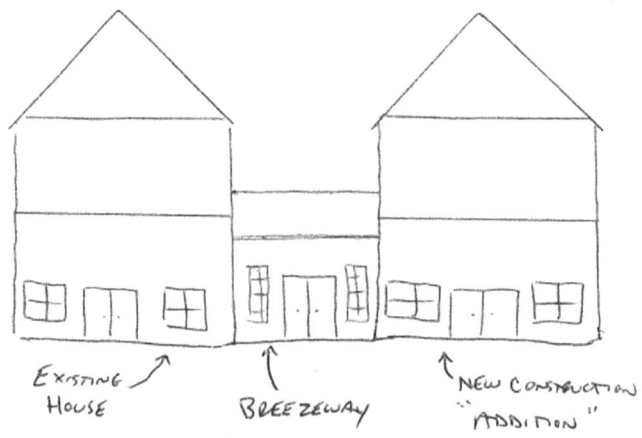

## Tiny Houses

A great idea in theory, however, economically they are generally not feasible within any built up urban area where people prefer such a housing type. The problem with tiny housing is that most jurisdictions in urban areas do not permit a house on wheels (tiny houses, RVs, tent trailers, etc.) as a principle dwelling, and the cost of the land in these areas would supersede the value of a permanent tiny house structure once its serviced, permitted, and built upon.

#TheHighestAndBestUse of tiny houses are to stack them on top of each other and call it a micro condo.

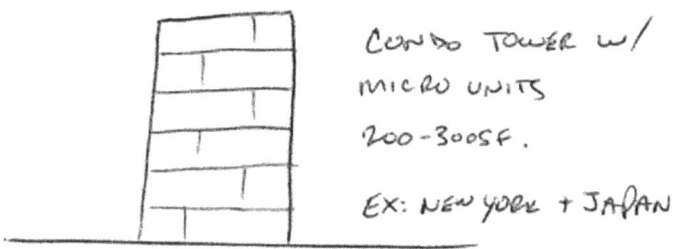

## Building on Stilts

In floodplain locations or seaside towns such as the "Outer Banks, North Carolina," the ocean tides and inclement weather are highly volatile during hurricane season. Building on stilts is the norm here, whereas building on stilts in London, England may be considered unusual. Geographic oddities in design are a form of #TheHighestAndBestUse.

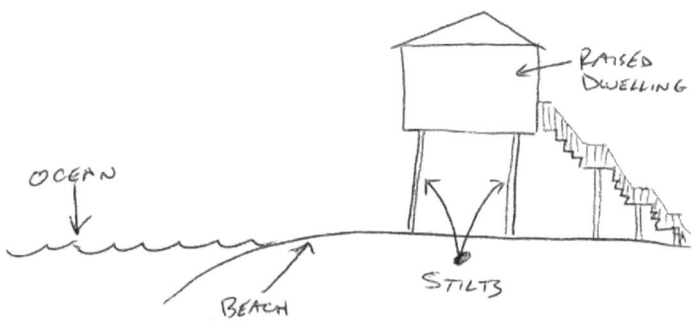

## Beams and LVLs

As a consideration, look at the cost for a structural modification vs. the value it generates. For example, a beam may cost $10,000 to purchase and install. Some may consider this "expensive" from a "dollars spent" standpoint. Now consider what that beam does for the space—does it allow open concept? Does it allow a second story to be constructed? Does it permit extra room in a basement for living space or a pool table? If that beam unlocks $30,000 worth of value down the road, how is "expensive" truly defined? #TheHighestAndBestUse.

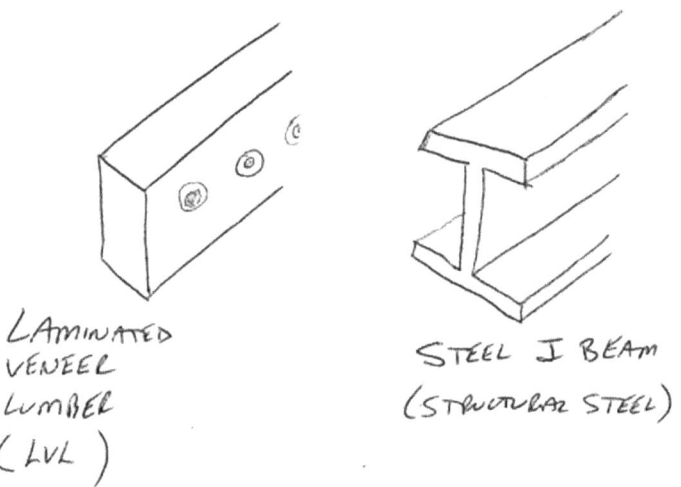

## 2.13 Unconventional Stories to Achieving Structural #TheHighestAndBestUse

*"The structure's interior remains largely vacant to this day as the windows are mostly shielded by advertisement."*

### Marketing Potential

At 1475 Broadway Avenue (also known as Times Square) in New York City, a building stands prominently overlooking one of the busiest street corners in America. Fifty million pedestrians visit Times Square annually coming to spend money, eat in restaurants, and see the bright lights.

*Chapter 2.00 : #TheHighestAndBestUse of the "Structure"*

*History*

At the south end of Times Square bordering four major street corners, a building affectionately labeled "The Times Tower" stands tall at 111m (363') above grade, twenty-five stories in total and was designed by Cyrus L. W. Eidlitz in 1904. In 1904, the *New York Times* newspaper constructed the building to house its media business until such time that it outgrew this space and moved in 1912. Between 1904 and 1912, the *New York Times* owner, Adolph Ochs, had lobbied the government of New York City to rename the area in front of the building "Times Square." This ended up being approved, and with all of the foot traffic this generated, a news ticker was installed for pedestrians at street level. In 1905, Adolph celebrated New Year's Eve with a rooftop fireworks display, drawing a crowd of 200,000 people to the area. This celebration continued until 1907, when he replaced the fireworks display with a large time ball (traditionally, this was a nautical device) that was lit to show the countdown on New Year's Eve. As the ball drop grew in popularity, it became a highly regarded tourist attraction of the city.

*Modern Day*

Years later in 1995, financial services firm Lehman Brothers acquired the Times Tower and began to research #TheHighestAndBestUse. They determined that the first couple floors may remain for commercial purposes as heavy foot traffic would demand, but the rest of the tower was far too costly to renovate vs. the income it would produce. Although interior renovations were too expensive, the income generation potential from signage was substantial, and from then on, the structure became one of the most prominent build boards ever known. General Motors, Discover Card, Nissin Foods, Dunkin Donuts, and Toshiba have all had advertisements on the building's facade. The structure's interior remains largely vacant to this day as the windows are mostly shielded by advertisement.

> **#TheHighestAndBestUse Quick Tip**
>
> *As a business owner, consider the cost vs. opportunity of owning a building in a high-traffic location. In the case of Times Square, the building would have had a previous economic value dictated by its original commercial rent roll. With an updated pro forma, that value is far superseded by an alternative use like signage because visitors are walking by. Someone thought differently about the positioning, and it paid off.*
>
> *In the case of a small business owner, with a shop, on a busy corridor, can you increase sales by updating your signage? Adding lights? Changing the direction it faces? Can you rent the sidewall of a corner lot building for other businesses' signage? #TheHighestAndBestUse.*
>
> *Cite 13*

### *Vertical Warehouse @ 33 Thomas Street, New York City*

There is a building at 33 Thomas Street in Manhattan, New York previously dubbed the AT&T Long Lines Building—this is a 170m (550') tall windowless skyscraper. Constructed in a precast facade, telephone companies required a building that was highly secure and close to the downtown core for their telephone operations, so they constructed a tower that was fireproof and able to resist nuclear fallout. Because land is so valuable in Manhattan, a vertical warehouse for telephone switching equipment with 16' ceilings and extra thick concrete floors was the most viable option. #TheHighestAndBestUse.

Cite 14

### *NYSE Stock Exchange/High Frequency Trading*

The NYSE Stock exchange headquarters in Manhattan at 46,000sf has been traded up for a 400,000sf location in New Jersey. This move was, in part, to accommodate several high frequency trading firms. Hyper-utilizing a trading term called "co-location," these trading firms seek a nanosecond edge over the next trader and, as such, pay huge sums of money to lease computer server racks in the same building that the stock exchange operates in.

These nanoseconds in trade timing can translate into millions of dollars when thousands of trades are happening every second on the open market. The closer the servers are to the trading switch, the faster they can communicate. According to Investopedia, it's said that even though the co-location servers are located in the same building as the exchange, these servers still receive the same length of wire that outside trading firms also receive to keep the market competitive.

At millions of dollars in annual rent, #TheHighestAndBestUse of this square footage might be to legally rent space to as many computer trading firms as possible.

Cite 14

# #TheHighestAndBestUse
# Golden Nuggets of "Structure"

*Chapter 2.00 : #TheHighestAndBestUse of the "Structure"*

*Chapter 3.00*

# #THEHIGHESTANDBESTUSE OF "YOUR SKILL SETS AND TIME"

*Chapter 3.00 : #TheHighestAndBestUse of "Your Skill Sets and Time"*

# INTRODUCTION

*"Time is the ultimate commodity. It cannot be bought, sold, traded, or given back."*

#TheHighestAndBestUse of your "skill sets and time" is the third major component to making the highest and best use system function for you. In this section we will dive into topics associated with sharpening your skills, identifying which real estate path might be best suited for you, and using time to its fullest potential.

For example, the "skill sets" of a basement apartment expert are vastly different than a seasoned developer parceling out a 50-acre farm, and a wholesaler dealing with off market sellers would not be the person to construct a hospital. The skill set requirements are just too far apart. Could that person get there? For sure. Will it happen overnight without some middle projects in between? Unlikely.

Your "time" as an entrepreneur will be considered the biggest investment in your career. Yes, even bigger than money. Time is the ultimate commodity. It cannot be bought, sold, traded, or given back. You can use other people's time, and you can use other people's skills, but your time as a business owner is finite and must be deployed with precision.

The goal for this chapter is to internally recognize where you're currently at, and which direction you want to head.

# 3.01 QUITTING YOUR JOB

*"It only makes sense to quit your job when it is costing you money, or something else of value, to stay where you are."*

**The "quit your job movement"** is such a hot button on social media these days. The online advertisement space is filled with "quit your job and start a business, "tell your boss he's an asshole," "TGIF," "another day another dollar." In blunt form, it only makes sense to quit your job when it is costing you money, or something else of value, to stay where you are. The same thing goes for hiring employees, changing your business strategy, or changing your business outlook. If you're doing something that is taking away from a better opportunity, make a change. Until then, what are you changing for?

For example, if you work a nine-to-five job to make $200 and during that same amount of time you could have sold fifteen widgets for a $20 net profit each ($300), you'd be costing yourself money to stay in that nine-to-five position and detracting from your "potential" business endeavors. However, it should be made very clear that a job provides you with a base level of day-to-day security, and a job should be considered one of the tools to get you closer to your goals. A self-employed person that's gunning for the $300 per day has more to consider like marketing, insurance, sales fulfillment, book keeping, employee management, etc.

If your short-term goal is to enjoy life and chill on the weekends, starting a business isn't for you. In this case, #TheHighestAndBestUse here is raising your employment value to your employer, which will land you a few extra bucks per hour, and that will provide a higher return on your time spent working there. Asking for a raise without giving the employer a consistently improved work ethic in advance is the same as the grocery store outright jacking up the price for canned soup. You'd say to the cashier, "What's changed? It's the same soup!?"

If starting a business is the direction you have decided to go, be sure to consider the time, money, risk, sleepless nights, working holidays, working weekends, industry drama, market fluctuations, overhead, staffing, upsides, and challenges that come along with it. If money is the main reason for your decision, and you can't reasonably forecast making at least double your nine-to-five net income by being self-employed, the juice isn't worth the squeeze.

In order to transition effectively, begin by working evenings and weekends on your idea until such time that it flourishes into something bigger. If and when you have a consistent horizon of opportunity that checks all the boxes mentioned above, that's when you should decide which direction to go. It's your 9:00 a.m. to 5:00 p.m. job that pays the bills, and it's your 5:00 p.m. to 9:00 a.m. job that gets you closer to those goals. Too many good employees have left their salaried positions to start a real estate business only to realize they did so too soon, can't qualify for bank financing anymore, and didn't have the training they thought they did.

Life is long, don't rush it.

## 3.02: Identifying and Changing Your Personal Growth Patterns

*"A job is something you work at, a business is something you grow."*
— Ari Gold, Entourage

**Deciphering what you're really good at and where your comfort zone lies should** be the first step to finding your constraints in business and in life. If you don't know yourself, then you can't know your business and your vision will lack clarity. There are several questions to ask yourself when venturing into the world of entrepreneurship, some of which are noted below. Take a minute to write down the answers, as these will be fundamental building blocks to consider moving forward.

*Identifying Questions:*

- How much time can you afford to spend away from your spouse, or your kids, or that person you are a primary caregiver for?
- How much stress can you handle if things go wrong?
- What is your financial situation like and how will it be impacted during the process?
- What is your network saying about you and who are the five closest people that you spend time with?
- Of those five people, what are their skill sets, what is their life like and what is their income bracket?
- Who can you call on if things don't go as planned to keep you in line?
- Have you done this before?
- How much time will this endeavor take for you to pull off from start to finish? (Be honest, this is a big one. The only person you cheat with a misguided answer is yourself.)
- How good are you at what you do?
- Is this your first of many projects, or a one-and-done?
- If it's the first of many, what is your future outlook?

- If this is a one-and-done, what is the learning curve attributed to understanding what is needed to be learned during the process? How does that affect your time and overall ROI?
- Consider doing a personality test: DISC test, Meyers Briggs, etc. Google these, they can be done online at little or no cost. These are excellent at identifying the way you are wired if you can't decipher if for yourself.

**Key Tips For Changing Your Personal Growth Patterns:**

*Read*

The top CEOs of the world read one to two books a month or more. You must read. This is the least expensive form of education. If saving money is your top priority, or you're just feeling the waters as to what type of real estate path might like, start here. Additionally, this is the best way to get quality information on a topic at your own pace.

*Mentorship*

Find someone that you're comfortable with that has been where you want to go. Pay that person to elevate your game. There is no fast track to success, but this is the closest thing. Spend money to save time.

*Podcast*

Listen to at least one full length podcast per week. This is often quality content that is targeted to the topic of your choice, with a guest speaker who is knowledgeable in that field.

*YouTube*

Listen or watch at least one YouTube video per day. There is zero cost in doing this.

*Making Use of Down Time*

Lying in bed or commuting to work is (in my opinion) downtime and is especially positive for soaking in new educational information. Audio books fit nicely here.

### Audio books

A variety of audio books relating to the topic you're looking to grow on. If it's real estate development, go there; if it's finding your why and life's purpose, go there. Audio books are a great way to taste different aspects of business and life and are highly portable. You don't leave home without your phone, so have a couple books on there at all times.

### Peer Groups

Join a real estate club in your area or online. There's a good chance that somebody has been down the path that you are looking to travel.

### Google Searches

A Google search is so unbelievably powerful. Pick a key topic, type it into Google, and without leaving your seat you have some good general knowledge on just about anything. Pages and pages and pages and pages of free stuff. First time home buyer checklist? Foreclosure/power of sale? Real estate agents in _____ city? Etc.

Remember, it's not the acquisition of knowledge that matters but the implementation of it that is most important. That's where experience doesn't cost, it pays.

**#TheHighestAndBestUse of Learning New Skills - Story**

*If you truly want to grow and build your business, you must take action and learn. As kids, we go to school and get educated on the various facets of life—geography, history, math, science, etc. This generic information is constructed to appeal to as wide an audience as possible. In real estate, we must hone in on the specifics that pertain to our individual situation.*

*My first property was a bank sale purchase on the MLS. This was a principal residence and although it wasn't a deep discount, it was cheaper than the norm and came with some personal benefits like two acres of land and a detached garage. This property needed work and had been neglected for years.*

*From a learning curve perspective, this is where my education began. Understanding construction, where to buy materials, how to transact a property, what it meant to get insurance—this was all new to me.*

*These skills were then rolled into the next property which was a fixer-upper basement apartment. The same items were used again here. Understanding construction, where to buy materials, how to transact a property, what it meant to get insurance...but this time, the skill of property management was added.*

*The succeeding properties continued to add even more skills like team building, time management, land development, flipping vs. rental, systems vs. hustle, etc., etc.*

*They say it takes 10,000 hours to become an expert at something. In a growth mode, you must be prepared to put in the time.*

*"Entrepreneurship is living a few years of your life like most people won't, so you can live the rest of your life like others can't."*— *Original Author Unknown*

## 3.03 SETTING OBJECTIVES

*"I read a book by professional poker player Phil Hellmuth…"*

**By setting objectives, also known as goal setting, you put down the fundamental** building blocks you need to create your best life and your best business. I like to break it down into two clearly defined areas: personal goals and business goals.

In this section, we will go through a simplified way to identify your goals. I like to keep things easy, streamlined, and efficient. Over the years, I've caught myself writing goals on multiple pieces of paper, in multiple databases, and over multiple emails. It's too difficult to keep track of all of your light bulb moments when they are located sporadically, so let's keep it to one simple spot.

*How to Get Started*
I read a book by professional poker player Phil Hellmuth on his preferred methods of goal setting. This book was called *#POSITIVITY* and I encourage you to read it. Some of the methods that are described here relate to the way that Phil discussed how he set goals for winning Las Vegas Poker Championship bracelets.

***Steps:***

1. Start by grabbing a sheet of paper for your business objectives and a sheet of paper for your personal objectives. Just standard lined paper, pen or pencil. This is a brainstorm session. Write down all the thoughts that you have for your personal and business objectives on each page respectively. Keep these objectives to condensed one-line thoughts, and remember nothing is off limits. Use a one-year time horizon.

2. For your personal objectives sheet, consider: Friends, family, sleep, enjoyment of life, kids, hobbies, extracurricular activities, health, and general well-being. For example, one of my objectives is to take casual weekend road trips in collectible cars (I happen to like cars). This has absolutely nothing to do with making money and has everything to do with enjoying life.

3. For your business objectives sheet, consider: Financial, distributing workload, scaling or shrinking your business, maximizing efficiency, new areas of expertise, education, marketing, sales, branding, acquisitions or dispositions, delegation, staffing. This has everything to do with the business as its own entity and where you want it to go.

4. Distill the personal and business objectives down to around eight to twelve items each. If you have too many objectives, it becomes too cluttered and will split your focus. You can expand and contract on these goals as you best see fit throughout the year. It's a living document and should be treated as such.

5. Every Monday morning, I recommend reading your objectives sheet to start the week. Hang them on your wall, or in the case of Phil Hellmuth, hang them on your bathroom mirror.

    Phil's mom hung objectives on the bathroom mirror as Phil grew up so that he, and all of his brothers, would see something to strive for on a daily basis. It was a large family that had one household bathroom, so they all had no choice but to read these for proper mental mindset at an early age.

    I like to read mine on Monday mornings because I feel it sets me up for the week.

6. Optional:

    I digitized my personal and business objectives in Photoshop onto a 12x24 branded poster board. Then, I found nice frames to place them in and rested a dry-erase marker on the top. From time to time if I feel the need to change something, I'll take the dry erase marker and write directly on the glass. You don't need to get too carried away with how it looks. It's quick and simple and can be done on the fly. Again, it's a living document, and your objectives on month two might be slightly different than month nine as you progress through the calendar year. That's ok. It's most important to establish a goal post, not the finish line. Place these somewhere where you will see them often.

*Recap:*

Brainstorm your objectives on a sheet of paper for personal and business, print and frame them after distilling down to eight to twelve items each, and hang on the wall. Read weekly.

> **#TheHighestAndBestUse Quick Tip**
> *Inspirational Quotes*
>
> *Inspirational quotes are the fundamental building block to success in many C-suite executives around the world. These ideals serve as gentle reminders to help guide their daily activities and leadership mindset in the right direction.*
>
> *A recommended action item is to print off some inspirational quotes and hang them on your office wall. For example, on my wall I have "Good Deals Are Found, Great Deals Are Created" and "Great Deals Happen When Terms Are More Important Than Price," among several others. Some quotes I came up with on my own. Some quotes are spoken by others. Just like your goal setting posters, frame these quotes in a similar manner and hang them somewhere visible..Review weekly to keep your head in the game.*

## 3.04 ROI, ROT, ROL (Return on Investment/Return on Time/Return on Life)

*"Money is 'binary.' Either you make it, or you lose it. It has no emotion."*
— *Kevin O'Leary*

**In this chapter, we discuss the difference between return on investment, return on** time, and return on life. (ROI, ROT, and ROL). Each has their place in an investor's career path, and each may vary depending on age, lifestyle, and business acumen. When reading this, think for yourself on what these items mean to your position in life.

### *Return on Investment*

ROI is financial—money in, money out. This generally relates back to how much you've spent on something vs. what is returned to you from that investment. For example, let's say you put $100,000 into a property and sold it for $115,000. That's an ROI of $15,000 or 15% (15K/100K = 15% ROI.

In the words of Kevin O'Leary from the TV show, *Dragons Den*, money is "binary." Either you make it, or you lose it. It has no emotion.

### *Return on Time*

ROT is time spent vs. results achieved. If your goal is to make a certain amount of money, quantify how long that will take. Is it to make $10,000 in one month? Or $10,000 in one year? Perhaps the goal is volume based. Is it to achieve five flips in five months or five principal residences in your entire lifetime?

In another perspective, ROT could be to achieve the same net income you currently earn but in 50% of the hours spent. ROT is how some business owners justify scaling their operations because it takes less of their time to operate the business once the systems are in place.

Often, time and money have an inverse relationship (save time, spend money) and time is the ultimate commodity. For example, a pay-per-use toll highway is not in the business of selling transportation, they sell <u>time</u>. Users travel along the paid road to cut down on distance, or traffic, or both. This always relates back to time.

### *Return on Life\**

ROL is what you do with your time and money for emotional purposes. Want a good life? Spend time or spend money on that thing you desire.

For example, I wanted a fireplace in our home. That came at significant financial cost. I said to myself, "That's a lot of money. I could make money with that money, and then reinvest again, and then…and then…" and then I realized that at some point you need to enjoy the fruits of your labour. I put the fireplace in.

Ask yourself: When is enough, enough? How do you evolve from one year to the next? How much money do you need to be happy? How many hours will that take? What does your personal and business life look like to define your efforts as successful? What does success look like to you?

*Paul D'Abruzzo

## 3.05 How to Decide When You Can't Decide

**When you can't decide on "something," it most often relates back to three primary** topics: Time, money, and emotional complexity. Assuming there are two choices, A or B, the decision to be made means that both options are equally challenging and could use a grading system to help separate what's holding you back. Ask yourself the questions below, and rank whether A or B is the best fit for you.

**Questions:**

Primary Motivation - Money? Time? Simplicity?
Best fit:

Dollars - Which one makes or loses most money?
Best fit:

Risk - Which one carries more risk? What are those risks?
Best fit:

Time - Which one takes the most/least amount of time input? Which takes longer in calendar days? Does that matter?
Best fit:

Skills - Do you have the skills to complete both tasks?
Best fit:

Timeframe – Short-term vs. long-term pain/pleasure.
Best fit:

Emotion - Which one would you prefer if time and money were no object?
Best fit:

Scale: How big do you want to take this? Push until you find your boundaries, then make a shift.(These boundaries are often financing, labour, material cost, market share, customer acquisition, etc.). Hit the limits, then adjust. (As a rule, pick the one that's most simple with the least moving parts. Emotional complexity is an energy vacuum, keep it simple.)

Best fit:

> **#TheHighestAndBestUse Quick Tip**
>
> *Something else to consider when making decisions:*
>
> *Good, cheap, or fast—**pick two**.*
>
> *Good and cheap - Won't be fast.*
> *Good and fast - Won't be cheap.*
> *Fast and cheap- Won't be good.*

## 3.06 Identifying Project Specific Skill Sets and Requirements

*"There is no ultimate success plan overall. There is only an ultimate success plan for you. It may or may not be the most money made or the least time spent—it's what you like the most. Period."*

**In this section, we will discuss #TheHighestAndBestUse** of a real estate case study and how the strategic approach to it may be affected depending on personal circumstance or personal skill set. In investing, the hypothetical lens at which a project is viewed will change from one investor's style to the next. In many investment circles, there is often a feeling of hierarchy that exists between single family/basement apartment investors, flippers, multifamily apartment owners, builders/developers, hedge fund or REIT operators, etc. These businesses are very similar, and drastically different, from one another.

It's a common thought that an investor may graduate from single-family homes to basement apartment conversions, to infill development, to then to being a big-time track builder or condo developer. While this has its merits, it's important to remember that there is no ultimate success plan overall, and there is only an ultimate success plan for you. It may or may not be the most money made or the least time spent—it's what you like the most. Period.

**Case Study:** *Land Severance and Existing House*

Using the example of a double wide residential lot, with some vacant land to one side and an existing fixer upper house on the other, we will identify the parameters about this deal in varying situations below, and then further identify which skill sets you must possess to successfully complete the related project. #TheHighestAndBestUse of a property for one person may be different than the next person, and we are about to find out why. To illustrate the point, Examples A -> L will serve as a guide.

*A) Buy and Hold with Future Construction Potential*

You've acquired the subject property and you're looking to build a portfolio of rental housing. You know that short-term income is good but long-term income is better. You're willing to wait out the short-term upside for long-term growth because in your view that's how you will win. The vacant land next door is a bonus because you may build there someday. For now, the vacant land sits as-is and the existing house will get renovated.

---

*Personal Requirements* (A)

Skill Sets - Beginner and Intermediate

Time Requirement - Some Time

Financing Required - Favourable for Long-Term Buy and Hold

Industry Connections Required - Mid Range

Motivation Level -Mid Range

Market Outlook - Positive

Strategic Market View - Long Term

## B) Teardown and Rebuild for Development

You're a developer. You have no interest in fixing an old house because you're into luxury markets. You want land and new construction, and you have an image to maintain. Your financing is private, which means the houses wouldn't carry long term. Your interior/exterior design skills are on point which helps drive more value to the structure, and that's how you win with your client base. Land value is irrelevant and as long as it is in the right area, you don't mind paying a premium because your buyer has an emotional attachment to your style of building.

> *Personal Requirements* (B)
> Skill Sets -Advanced
> Time Requirement - Lots of Time
> Financing Required -Favourable for Short-Term Flipping, All Cash
> Industry Connections Required - Extensive
> Motivation Level - Burning
> Market Outlook - Positive
> Strategic Market View - Short Term

## C) The Newbie Wholesaler

You're brand new to the industry. You just took a weekend course and now you're attempting wholesaling real estate. The subject property is tied up under contract and you have one friend who dabbles in properties like this. You have no financing, very little liquid cash, and want to move out of your parent's house. You want to get started in the industry.

> *Personal Requirements* (C)
> Skill Sets -Beginner
> Time Requirement - Some Time
> Financing Required - None
> Industry Connections Required - A Few, Mid Range
> Motivation Level -Mid Range, Burning
> Market Outlook - Neutral
> Strategic Market View - Short Term

### D) Cautious but Experienced Investor

You're an experienced investor who's never done new construction before. You got stuck in a downturn economy, fixed up the existing house to rent it, and now realize there's going to be a cash crunch coming down the pipe. The buy and hold side of the portfolio is good but you don't want to jeopardize your family's lifestyle in the short term for a long-term play, and that, truthfully, may take a long time to realize. Your industry contacts are phenomenal, and you're pretty sure you could pull this deal off, but the unknowns of construction are eating you up.

> *Personal Requirements* (D)
> Skill Sets -Advanced
> Time Requirement - Some Time
> Financing Required - Favourable for Long-Term Buy and Hold, Favourable for Short-Term Flipping
> Industry Connections Required - Extensive
> Motivation Level - Burning
> Market Outlook - Negative
> Strategic Market View - Short Term

## E) Experienced Builder That Overpaid

You're an experienced builder that knows they overpaid for the subject property. You realize that the existing house can be converted to a showroom (which is of benefit for your construction financing), and the vacant land would be an ideal show home. You own vacant land somewhere else in town, and even though you're overpaying for the subject property, this other vacant land has some tremendous upside. Your plan is to build a show home on the subject property's vacant land, use the showroom next door to lock in new clients for build sites, then sell the subject property at a loss. Your highest and best use was to piggyback one deal over the other because the aggregate of all deals combined is extremely positive for your timeline and financing needs.

---

*Personal Requirements* (E)

Skill Sets - Advanced

Time Requirement - Lots of Time

Financing Required - Favourable for Short-Term Flipping, All Cash,

Industry Connections Required - Extensive

Motivation Level - Burning

Market Outlook - Positive

Strategic Market View–Short Term, Long Term

---

## F) Full Scale Development of Boutique Commercial/Residential Project

You realize the zoning of the subject property is ideal for a mixed use boutique commercial/residential project. The land may be vacant on one half but the house on the other half could be torn down for a wider footprint. By taking down the house, you unlock a parking aisle, some landscape open space, and revisit the city bylaw for some minor variance exemptions. This project is a massive undertaking but you know the upside is huge and over the next seven years will become the hottest part of town. Short term, the interest cost will keep you up at night, but long term the deal would change your life in a big way. You proceed with the project and crush it.

> *Personal Requirements* (F)
> Skill Sets - Advanced
> Time Requirement - Lots of Time
> Financing Required - Favourable for Long-Term Buy and Hold, Favourable for Short-Term Flipping, All Cash
> Industry Connections Required - Extensive
> Motivation Level - Burning
> Market Outlook - Positive
> Strategic Market View - Long Term

### G) Full Scale Development of Boutique Project - Sold Early

You reviewed the project in example F, and realized that the development was great, but construction wasn't for you. You sell the vacant land, pre developed, and skip the construction because it's too stressful. This yielded you less upside but you learned a lot and can move on to the next project. Your mental health is worth more than the dollars.

> *Personal Requirements* (G)
> Skill Sets - Advanced
> Time Requirement - Some Time
> Financing Required - Favourable for Short-Term Flipping
> Industry Connections Required - Mid Range
> Motivation Level - Mid Range, Burning
> Market Outlook - Neutral, Positive
> Strategic Market View - Short Term

### H) The Land Assembly Play

On the subject property, the existing house is fixed up for now, and the vacant land will be left sitting there for ten years. It's dead equity, but the rest of the houses on the street are big lots and could be taken down at some point. Slowly, but surely, you acquire each property as they come available. The financing situation here is a long-term view, and you have some cash in the bank. Rather than flipping house after house, you wait for opportunities to come to you. It's only a matter of time before your one to two lots, turns into the newest land assembly in town, which combined is worth three times more than the lots were purchased for individually.

> *Personal Requirements* (H)
> Skill Sets -Intermediate Advanced
> Time Requirement - Some Time, Lots of Time
> Financing Required - Favourable for Long-Term Buy and Hold, All Cash
> Industry Connections Required - Mid Range
> Motivation Level - Low, Mid Range
> Market Outlook - Positive
> Strategic Market View - Long Term

## I) *The Inheritance and Impatient Investor*

You hate tenants, love money, hate construction and are impatient. This property came to you by family inheritance, and you can't stand the sight of it. There is no mortgage on this pig, and you have to pay the tax bill shortly. Get it out of here, you want to move on.

> *Personal Requirements* (I)
> Skill Sets -Beginner
> Time Requirement - Less Time
> Financing Required -Non-Available
> Industry Connections Required - A Few
> Motivation Level - Burning
> Market Outlook - Negative
> Strategic Market View - Short Term

*Chapter 3.00 : #TheHighestAndBestUse of "Your Skill Sets and Time"*

### J) Small Business Liquidity with Lifestyle Requirements

There are more deals than you can handle. Your business is a small Mom-and-Pop with a couple staff, and you know the bank will cut you on mortgage borrowing soon. Taking the first twenty cents of every dollar will have to be the way to go because you just can't hold every property long term, and the deals will come and go faster than you can team-build. You wholesale the properties for some short-term cash, do zero renovations, and get excessively liquid. The excess funds will help support the medical problem you know are lurking in the family, and it means less stress for you in the short term. Lifestyle is important.

---

*Personal Requirements* (J)
Skill Sets -Intermediate
Time Requirement - Less Time
Financing Required–Non-Available
Industry Connections Required - A Few Mid Range
Motivation Level - Mid Range
Market Outlook - Neutral
Strategic Market View - Short Term

---

### K) The Family-Oriented Investor

You're a wealthy family man/woman who wants to show your kid's work ethic. The subject property will take some considerable elbow grease, and you don't care if it makes money or not, but your kids need to learn what it's like to roll up their sleeves and get dirty because the value of mindset is more important than the value of dollars. Paint, flooring, and kitchen renovations aren't your forte but it will be a bonding experience.

> *Personal Requirements* (K)
> Skill Sets - Beginner
> Time Requirement - Some Time
> Financing Required - Favourable for Short-Term Flipping, All Cash
> Industry Connections Required - A Few
> Motivation Level - Low Mid Range
> Market Outlook - Neutral
> Strategic Market View - Short Term

**L) The Smart Upstart Investor**

You buy the subject property knowing that you don't know everything, but you do know a bit about a lot, and that's good enough to get the ball rolling. Financing is reasonable for short-term flips or long-term buy and holds. You're liquid enough to take on a problem if/when it happens. This type of play will help your brand as a local investor, and you take on a coach to help you get over the hump. Short term, it makes sense. Long term, it has upside. The coaching will get you to where you need to be.

> *Personal Requirements* (L)
> Skill Sets - Beginner
> Time Requirement - Some Time
> Financing Required - Favourable for Long-Term Buy and Hold, Favourable for Short-Term Flipping
> Industry Connections Required - A Few
> Motivation Level - Mid Range
> Market Outlook - Positive
> Strategic Market View - Short Term, Long Term

As the examples have demonstrated, everybody has a different experience and different skill level when it comes to real estate. The fact that the same property can have so many different viewpoints is truly amazing. That's the power of real estate—it can be rented, renovated, transformed, transferred, or transacted. Think critically about your deals because it's not about what other people think of you or your business, it's about what you think of yourself.

> #### #TheHighestAndBestUse - Story
>
> *For a brief moment early in my real estate career, I got off track, doing too much of what other people said I should do. I was a busy entrepreneur, fixing and renting properties, and from time to time I overspent on what everyone else thought was a good idea.*
>
> *Real estate agents have one opinion: "Fix the shingles" or "replace all the windows," they would say. Investors had another opinion, "Do as little as you can to the property, it's just a rental." Here I was somewhere in the middle trying to make everyone happy because I thought that's what I was supposed to do. It was then that I realized that the best advice is received from an expert in the industry, with no skin in the game.*
>
> *Putting new windows in a house might cost $20,000, but it may only raise the value of the house by that same amount. That's net neutral to the investor, and a potential waste of your time and capital if there isn't any upside upon completion. If a tenant is telling you to put in new windows, perhaps it's to save them money on utilities. If an agent is telling you to put in new windows, perhaps it's because they make more money as a percentage of the final price sold and not the net value lift in your pocket. If the neighbour is telling you to put in new windows, maybe it's because they want to sell their property next year, and the higher sale price will benefit them indirectly.*
>
> *Always put your objectives in perspective, and remember that you must be deliberate with your intentions to achieve what you consider #TheHighestAndBestuse of your own success.*

## 3.07 Business Style Identification Flow Chart

*"Remember, there is no "Right Answer," only what's "Right For You, Right Now."*

**In this chapter, we identify real estate investment business streams in point form.** If you are strong in a particular category and skill set, or weak in another, this may help you choose which direction to trend toward. Remember, there is no "right answer," only what's "right for you, right now."

Something to strongly consider is the operational drag that is associated with each of the following disciplines. Operational drag for business application is defined by how much back end support or front end effort is required to make something function.

**Wholesaling**

Marketing → Acquisition → Client Management/Transactional Management → Disposition

Wholesaling is largely sales and marketing based where the "product" is real estate and is sold privately to a buyer's list before the contracted closing day. This is often referred to as the business of "distressed assets." Liquidations, cars, houses, jewelry, etc. are all markets based on this principle, and function by solving someone's problem. This stream is all based on timing of finding the right seller/buyer at the right time.

**Wholetailing**

Marketing → Acquisition → Transactional Management → Financing → Cleanup/Cleanout → MLS Disposition

Similar to wholesaling, wholetailing is largely sales and marketing based where the "product" is real estate, and is sold on the open market through real estate agents. Buy low, sell low, and done on the MLS.

**Flipping**

Marketing → Acquisition → Transactional Management → Financing → Construction → MLS Disposition

Flipping is more marketing and construction based, often with an MLS resale to an end user buyer. Some flippers acquire from wholesalers, while others do their own acquisitions through marketing. The property's finishes are typically upgraded when flipping takes place.

**Buy and Hold**

Marketing → Acquisition → Transactional Management → Financing → Construction →Refinancing→ Property Management and Maintenance→ Disposition

Buy and hold investing is more marketing, construction, and management based. If you acquire a property off market, this takes on every role noted in the flipping/wholesaling world, plus the efforts to "create" a rentable property from the existing housing stock. If the property is rented for long-term wealth creation, tenants will occupy the space, which requires property management and ongoing annual maintenance. Single family homes, rent to own/lease to own, and multiunit apartment strategies would also fit into this category. Buy and hold properties can be sold on the MLS or privately, sometimes with a vendor take back mortgage to incentivize the buyer and reduce income tax payments.

Note: not all properties need to be found privately, but that method does often bring the best purchase price.

**Development (Developer)**

Land acquisition → Land Planning Applications → Approvals/Disapprovals → Pre-Servicing → Disposition Of Lots

Development is more procedural and largely paper based real estate. From land acquisition to the disposition of serviced lots, this can take years of careful planning, and execution. Sometimes, lots will be sold privately, and sometimes through MLS retail channels. Also, sometimes a developer may postpone collecting a full payout to show good faith to the builder until the structures have been constructed and sold in full.

**New Construction (Builder)**

Presale of Homes → Construction → Disposition (Resale) or Refinance (Long-Term Hold)

A builder is the construction phase of new construction. This is the part that the general public visually sees and is the final step to the new construction process. Once built, the dwellings are most often liquidated in the open market through MLS or private marketing channels like an onsite sales center. In the case of purpose built rental housing, a mortgage may be placed on the properties by the builder to maintain ownership in perpetuity.

**Real Estate Sales Professional**

Marketing → Customer Acquisition → Purchase or Sale of Property → Repeat

A real estate sales professional (also called a realtor, an agent, a sales representative) is someone who transacts real property on the open market (MLS), or privately between buyer and seller, through a brokerage for a commission or flat fee. There are several services available that offer low commission, high commission, white glove service, and every option in between. If a sales agent is part of a larger brokerage, that agent would pay a portion of their commissions to that brokerage. Agents are traditionally compensated as a percentage of the final sale price.

## 3.08 SCALING AND DELEGATION

*"I'd rather have 1% of a 100 people's efforts, than 100% of my own."*
— *John D Rockefeller*

**Positioning your efforts for success** is one of the key points that every entrepreneur, CEO, and business owner must drill down on in order for their business to flourish. Your business is your baby and if you want to see your baby succeed you will need to place a disproportionate amount of time and mental capacity in the right areas. If you want your efforts to be working towards #TheHighestAndBestUse, you need to double down on your creativity and do something that the next person isn't or find an existing process and do it better. Remember, there's no easy money anywhere, and every business has its own set of nuances.

### Delegation

"You can only have one to two jobs maximum, but you can have 1,000 vending machines working for you around the clock." ~ Source Unknown

This is one of the most legitimate quotes I've ever read. I think it was a social media post a while back that was floating around and it really stuck with me. A vending machine has no emotion, doesn't care if you're sleeping or awake, and as long as it's plugged in, managed effectively, and in a high-traffic area, you'll be making money.

There are two ways to delegate effort in your business. One is people, the other is technology. To illustrate this point, we will turn back to history.

In the 1950s, computer technology was comparatively poor vs. today's standards and there was really no opportunity to outsource certain tasks in any other manner but human labour. Photocopiers like a Xerox machine were at their infancy, so people transcribed or created printing dies for recreation. In similar fashion, look at the "Bell Telephone" network. At one time, there was a human patching in cables from one area of the grid to another. A telephone user on one end would pick up the phone and call the operator switchboard, at which point that user would request the recipient's "line." The operator would then physically connect a wire from A to B. Times have changed. Now, you hammer in the other person's phone number and voila! From anywhere in the world, they pick up. I can only imagine the uproar that took place when Bell got rid of these thousands of women (and yes they were mostly women) and displaced their positions with technology. The same thing probably held true for the blacksmith/horse and buggy industry when companies like The Chevrolet Brothers, Rolls-Royce, and countless others showed up on the scene with gasoline engines.

Delegation is one of the biggest keys to successful business. You must delegate your tasks to employees with skills seven out of ten, and above. You can't scale a business on fours, it doesn't work. These folks take too much management to economically produce output. Your hires should be able to solve things for you once trained, if not, they must be replaced. The best employees "anticipate."

**Scaling to Substantiate the Cost of Hiring**

Businesses require a certain size of operation in order to substantiate the cost of hiring staff. If you are a one-man band, you reap all the financial rewards, carry all the risks, and do all the work. Also, if you are sick or on vacation, business stops. For all businesses, there is a critical mass at which you must attain to make the hiring process function effectively.

*"The Apple Cart" Example*

Let's assume that you have an apple cart and you are the sole proprietor. You stand by your cart at the side of the road selling apples one by one as cars pull over. Bag, after bag, after bag, you greet the customers, take the payment, and restock the shelves. After a while, selling apples one by one is no longer exciting you, so you open a second apple cart. The next steps you take would be to hire somebody to operate that apple cart in another high traffic location, while you run the original cart. Some simple economics of growth have taken place as outlined below in the chart.

**Cost Plus**

Volume has increased in apple sales +$
Market share and brand visibility increase +$
Volume discount on raw materials (apples) +$

**Cost Minus**

Bookkeeping has increased due to higher volume and higher retail activity -$
Staff now require updated company liability insurance -$
Staff now require workman compensation insurance -$
Staff now require payroll source deductions and a payroll service -$
Purchase of additional overhead (x1 apple cart) -$
Lease of additional retail space (rent) -$
Maintenance and repair of the cart (paint, signage) -$
Employee theft and/or spoilage -$
Marketing budget Increases -$
Hourly wages -$

In the real world, it's fairly linear and a low entry-cost exercise to go build an apple cart for a couple thousand bucks as a solopreneur, have some apples dropped off and sit by the side of the road. The owner could probably cover off on any of the extra expenses by doing their own books, hanging their own signage, and doing their own payroll. But if we scale to twenty-five apple carts then things get a little bit more complicated.

As you scale, you can no longer rely on the tactics of you as a sole operator and #TheHighestAndBestUse of your time becomes operating on strategy vs. that of your physical effort. This means brain power. This means arithmetic. This means creativity. This means you have to build a business around all of the key facets such as sales, marketing, supply, and demand, and so on. There are economic dead zones in scaling a business where the cost of management supersedes the gains achieved by previous level of volume. For this, the Fibonacci sequence prevails.

**The Fibonacci Sequence**

The Fibonacci sequence is a naturally occurring mathematical formula that mother nature uses to grow cells on planet earth. A plant's leaf structure most often multiplies in this model, as do small businesses, and it works as follows. According to the *Oxford Dictionary*, "The Fibonacci sequence is a series of numbers in which each number (*Fibonacci number*) is the sum of the two preceding numbers. The simplest is the series 1, 1, 2, 3, 5, 8, 13, 21, 34, etc."

Put simply, 1+1=2,2+1=3,3+2=5,5+3=8, and so on. Barring specific intricacies within the business, a company would need to hire in a similar fashion in order to justify the cost of scaling the business and the overhead associated with that.

For example, a three-employee company would be fairly easy for an owner operator to manage. That owner is in direct control of the day to day and is familiar with the happenings. But when they outgrow the third staff member, now they need management. The cost of the management is fixed (one person's salary), so they may need to jump from three staff to five or eight employees in order to maintain profitability. If the sales volume remains the same as a three employee model, there is a good chance that all of the financial gains of previous profitability will be wiped out by the salary of that fourth individual (three employees and one manager).

You can see we are now in between Fibonacci sequence numbers at four, and the short-term cost is greater than the profit. In order to bring those numbers back in line, the sales must grow disproportionately to the expense of adding that fourth person. With more sales, comes more logistics, and more logistics requires more help. There is an equilibrium point that is reached where sales volume and effort required balance off, and this is typically at a Fibonacci number. As a general rule, an employee should generate three times their salary in gross sales to profitably justify their position.

Like we talked about above, with scale means that you have to rely on strategy to fulfill the businesses (sales and marketing) and not "brute force" of working extra hours to get over the hump. This requires vision, vision requires budget, budget requires volume, and around and around we go.

A great additional resource on growing a small business is a book by Michael Gerber called *The E Myth Revisited*.

*Considerations to Ask Yourself Before Scaling Your Business:*
- Available Market Share
- Brand Visibility
- Spin Off Businesses
- Future Growth
- Succession Planning

- Industry Clout and/or Ego
- Volume for Other Sub Business Benefits
- Positing for Liquidation of the Business
- Industry Contacts
- Volume Discounts/Economies Of Scale
- Upside Potential vs. Downside Risk Protection
- Global Economic Factors
- Recession Protection/Too Big to Fail
- "Opportunity Breeds Opportunity" Mentality
- Time Considerations/Personal Involvement Pre-Scaling
- Time Considerations/Personal Involvement Post-Scaling

## 3.09 Profits: Fixed Costs vs. Variable Costs

*"Return on time and profit margin always have a relationship."*

**I should mention that I'm not the expert on scaling a large enterprise as I've kept** my business relatively lean, but I'll share some opinions on the topic that are prudent to growing and that others have taught me along the way.

Scaling a business requires exponential staff as it grows. A restaurant with only takeout dining would require a small kitchen, one to two cooks, and a cashier. They could handle X number of orders per day.

If the restaurant wanted growth, and added twenty-one tables, they would need to hire a front-of-house host, another chef, a larger POS system, increased accounting, a dedicated dishwasher, larger interior footprint (and rent), additional freezer space, and one to two more servers. The challenge of twenty-one tables is that in many cases it doesn't justify the added expense of all of these additional items because the cost of those items are riding on the backs of just twenty one tables. The business may end up negative vs. staying lean and efficient.

In order to justify the expense of scaling, the restaurant may need to add thirty-four to fifty-five tables so as to spread the expense load across more income generating opportunities. (Think of each table like a mini-business.) These are the fundamentals of "fixed cost vs. variable cost."

## *Fixed Costs*

Fixed costs identify as something that needs to be paid regardless of if you sell something or not. Something like rent would be a fixed cost, and it must be paid whether you are open for business or closed for the season. Fixed costs in a real estate business may include: the cost to incorporate, an unlimited bandwidth internet connection, nationwide cell phone plan, property taxes, annual insurance, etc.

## *Variable Costs*

Variable costs are expenses that move with the volume of sales you're doing. For example, a small restaurant may order 100 hamburger patties per month. A large restaurant may order 500 patties per month. The average cost of these patties may go down by ordering larger volumes because of bulk order discounts or savings on delivery fees.

Variable costs in a real estate business may include: seasonal utility usage, pay-per-use property management software, accounting and bookkeeping (based on transactional volume), income-proportionate commercial liability insurance, building materials (commodity based), fuel, employee wages, etc.

Increasing variable costs are common with all physical labour businesses that plan to grow their sales. The overhead grows with it. In a digital agency style business, the variable cost model changes because your overhead of execution remains the same (fixed), but the output can grow at unlimited potential. For example, digital marketing requires a person or system to post the ad on a social media platform once, select the ad spend related to how often they want people to see it, and out it goes. Whether it's a $100 ad spend at 10 views, or $10,000 ad spend with thousands of views, the effort to get it working on the platform is the same.

Compare one-click social media advertising to dancing human billboards promoting a local muffler shop. Social media is a far more efficient way to capture attention, at a streamlined cost.

## Profit Margins

As you grow your business, remember to consider your profit margins. For example, let's say a small and efficient business is making 20% net margin on $500,000 gross sales ($100,000 net). If the business owner scales the operation to double their volume to $1,000,000 in sales, and in the process reduces the margin to 10%, the net financial position is the same ($100,000 net).

If the goal is to five times the business within three to five years to be recognized as an industry brand, the reduced margin and interim minutia are just a stepping-stone on the way to the top. If the end goal is growing sales for a stronger net income, is it worth it? More volume doesn't always mean more net income.

Something else to consider would be the business owners return on time at different levels of scale. In the first example of a 20% net margin and $500,000 in sales, we need to contemplate the time input of the business owner. Is the business owner working 2,000 hours per year to achieve the net $100,000? If the business has grown to double the sales at $1,000,000, perhaps the margins are reduced (10%), but is the business owner working 650 hours per year to achieve the same previous income?

Ex:
$500,000 Gross Sales x 20% Net Margin = $100,000 Net Income / 2000 Hours = $50/hour

Ex:
$1,000,000 Gross Sales x 10% Net Margin = $100,000 Net Income / 650 Hours = $153/hour.

These are pros and cons that must be worked out. Return on time and profit margin always have a relationship. And since we can't scale a business on four out of ten (only sevens plus), there needs to be an incentive for the business owner to take on more risk for the same amount of income. In this example, it's return on time, and the management that handles the increase in sales volume would be making day-to-day decisions. If there's no more time, or no more money, the risk position increases and the rewards are diminishing.

## What Is Everyone Else Doing - Story

*There was a point in my career where I got caught up in what other people were doing and began using them as an emotional measuring stick for my own operations. I remember sitting in seminars thinking, "How does this person do so much volume" or "How does this person do so many sales per year?" At the time, I didn't fully look into what sales numbers actually meant, or what net profit was being generated at the end of the day.*

*It got me down, it made me question what I had been doing for the last number of years, and frankly it made me sad. Following this, I started doing some research.*

*For the investors out there claiming to do hundreds of deals, what did that look like under the hood? For local construction experts doing hundreds of thousands of dollars in renovations, what did that look like?*

*Through a unique chain of events, I ended up having a great conversation about this with somebody who was also an entrepreneur in the business, and he put it to me like this. He said, "Ryan, you never know what's happening behind the scenes, you never know what that person's life is like, you never know what their family is like, you never know where they started to where they've come to today, you don't know their bottom line, you just don't know. Don't compare yourself to anybody else, play your own game."*

***************************

### Margin vs. Downsizing - Story

*I sat down for dinner with an individual operating a publicly successful business in the construction industry. I had seen this individual speak at some conferences in the past, and they had been doing about $20,000,000 in gross annual sales. I admired this person, a go-getter entrepreneur doing high volume in a crowded market.*

*Something that came out naturally over the course of this meal was a 6% net margin over the 20 million in sales, which works out to a $1.2 million dollar net income to the business. Some people may think, "Wow, $1.2 million, that's fantastic," and they'd be right. That's huge money. but then I got to thinking to myself, 1.2 million over 20 million in sales with all of those moving parts, risk, and overhead, 6% net margin, isn't that thin?*

*At a later date, the industry had shifted and I heard this person had downsized their operations by approximately half, increased their operating margin, and therefore decreased the risk. Very smart move. This was all due to reducing the scale of the business. I learned a lot from this and have tremendous respect for the business owner.*

*"What you lose in margin, you gain in volume," and for that you must find an equilibrium.*

# 3.10 MARKUP VS. MARGIN: THEY AREN'T THE SAME

*"Price is what you pay, value is what you get" ~ Author Unknown*

**There is a clear difference between markup and margin that many business owners** tend to get confused on. In this example, we will use a product such as lumber to explain markup, and then we will cross reference all of the markup into the margin of a business.

For example, if you buy lumber for $10 and mark that lumber up by 15% to your customer, $10.00 x 1.15 = $11.50 invoiced. Your markup is $1.50.

To find margin, take your profit ($1.50) and divide that by the total sale. $1.50 / $11.50 = 13%.

What we've now established is that your markup on materials is 15% and the total margin on the sale is 13%. To work this out on your business as a whole, you need to add up your total sales, subtract your operating expenses, and you will end up with net profit, that can be divided by gross sales for the final net operating margin.

Ex:
Total sales: $500,000.
Total material expenses: -$240,000
Total Overhead/Labour: -$230,000
Net Profit: +$30,000

Net Margin: $30,000/$500,000 = 6%

If your margin is 6% and your industry operates at 2%, you're a rock star. If you're margin is 6% and your industry operates at 14%, some tweaks need to be made in the process to cut costs or drive more value to the customer. The reason margin is so important is because companies strategize their business plans based on gross sales and expenses in aggregate, not on how much each individual item gets marked up to a customer.

*Cutting Costs vs. Adding Value:*
There are two defined ways that you can improve your business operating margins. The first way is to cut costs and is the most common way for an accountant to tell you how to run a more profitable business. The second way to improve your margin is to increase the value to the customer, which is the most common way for a sales person to enhance the bottom line. We will discuss #TheHighestAndBestUse of both methods.

*Cutting Costs*
Cutting costs could be doing something simple like changing raw material suppliers. Some long-standing relationships end up in the weeds because the product supplier gets comfortable with the buyer, or the buyer stops checking comparable prices of the competitor because it's easier to maintain the status quo. Always cross compare.

Another way to cut costs would be to fire people. There's no nice way to say it—firing staff means less overhead. At the end of the day, a business needs a certain number of key people to operate, and outright axing the people that you thought you needed to begin with may or may not be the solution. Weigh it out.

Other ways to cut costs:

- Updating to new computer software
- Updating current technologies within the business such as databases and customer relationship management software
- Changing marketing channels (exit print, enter social media)
- Updated bookkeeping or accounting process (receipt management and automation)
- Adjustments for less air travel and more video conference
- Outsourcing components vs. producing in house
- Virtual assistant vs. in-office assistant

*Adding Value*

Adding value is a best practice way to grow your business because it's forward thinking and it provides more service to companies or individuals that are seeking what you offer. You can raise the bridge or lower the river, but if you're in a service provider industry, the last thing you want somebody to do is cut your price after you've gone through and done a proposal.

If you're a contractor, having somebody undercut your bid by $2,000 is tough because you put so much time and effort into getting "this close." If you're a real estate agent, losing a deal by 0.25% commission cut is heartbreaking because the market is very competitive. In cases like this, hold your price firm and over index on the service delivered. Real estate agents offering photos, staging, yard cleanup, interior paint touch ups, 3D tours, drone photography, or duct cleaning would be a great place to start. These are lower ticket items that may help the client move forward with your services, and they are outsourced to other companies for a solid return on your time.

"Price is what you pay, value is what you get," and if someone didn't buy your offer, it's because they felt the value was too low for the price being paid.

## 3.11 Types of Roles in a Company: #TheHighestAndBestUse of Staff

*"Be a leader, not a boss. Find employees that anticipate."*

**There are several mindsets and personality types that one can hire for their** organization. Below, we discuss some of those positions and how they may integrate with your company's direction. Remember, not all jobs are income producing (directly), some are net neutral and some are support staff. Those support roles are generally structured to free up your time/other employee's time, to do something that is, in fact, income producing.

In addition to finding the right people, I recommend you build a company around a clear market opportunity by focusing on your strengths and hiring your weaknesses. A great way to do this is have your new hires complete a personality test as part of the hiring process. DISC test, Meyers Briggs, or several others available for low or no cost are available with a quick Google search. Some roles that may fit those results are described herein.

**The Visionary**

This person is the tip of the spear, the dreamer, the top of the funnel, and the "ideas" behind the operation. Oftentimes the visionary is the business owner. The business owner takes creative thought, converts that thought to task-worthy actions, and then executes on a plan. This person gives direction to the organization from a high level in a large company, or as someone who does the execution in a DIY fashion. Many small businesses will start as DIY with one employee (the visionary) and grow from there.

**The Do'er**

This is the down n' dirty person that gets shit done. Need to build a house? Need some landscaping? Need some physical labour? Need to move stuff? This is the person. They are often motivated by task related goals and love to see progress. Because they think this way, they may have weaknesses in other areas like organization. Do'ers are needed on the team and they focus on the how.

**The Organizer**

This is often management, or the behind-the-scenes type of person. They think in logistics, they think in efficiency, they think while others are actively doing task based related items on the production front. Accounting, clerical work, engineering, traffic control—these are all organizational mindsets that do'ers need to keep the wheels on the bus.

**The Locker Room Person**

Some people are just great spirits. They are sometimes (but not always) unproductive or unskilled on the job, but motivate the heck out of everyone around them. This is "the locker room" personality. They are always in a good mood, happy go lucky, jolly old goof that keep the morale up and coffee flowing. Hockey teams hire people like this, just the same as in the 90s they hired enforcers to fend off ruffians from their most skilled athletes. I worked on the assembly line at General Motors while I was a student. The job was so-so most of the time, but one day I had a chance to work with the happiest and most hilarious guy I'd ever met. The day flew by, big smiles. This is where I learned the power of a "locker room" person.

**Inherent Optimist/Inherent Pessimist**

There is room in your business for these types of people every day of the week. There are folks that feel the world is their oyster and they can do no wrong. Everything is an opportunity waiting to happen and there is no such thing as negativity. There are also the daily pessimistic types where the world is against them and nothing will work out. The "only thing in life that's a guarantee is death and taxes" type. These personality traits are a fantastic tool to vet your deals.

Example, you are looking at a property and wonder what could be amazing or what could go wrong. You take this deal to both these people and ask them to make a list. Within twenty minutes, you'll now have the sunshine rainbow lollipop list and also one from the depths of hell. As a business owner, weigh the options and see what's going to work best for you.

**Advisory Staff**

Advisory staff such as legal, finance, venture capital, or "the gray hair" on your team are excellent ways for you to vet your decisions from people who may have been in your shoes some time ago. Something to consider here is where the advice is coming from within and why they are saying it now. Is this the advice they wish they had when they were in your position? Is it hearsay? Have they actually experienced this? Is this the best advice for them, or for you?

## 3.12 Treating Your Staff With Respect/Company Culture

*"Invest in education with profits from your business.  
Then reinvest in your business by investing in people."*

**Best explained by a couple stories, the underlying fundamental way to scale your** business and create #TheHighestAndBestUse of your team's efforts are to build the company culture. No culture? No future. I make an explicit point to care about my staff on a repeat basis whether it's with compliments, gifts, outings to somewhere that they wouldn't have taken themselves, time off, surprise visits, job site coffees, or similar. This isn't manipulation or some tactic that was discussed on a YouTube video—this is real people caring for real people. "People don't remember what you said, or what you did, but they remember how you made them feel." Words to live by.

**Wynn Resorts Story**

Steve Wynn, one of Las Vegas' largest casino operators and most notorious developers, is well known in the media for treating his staff with exceptional care. A reporter once asked Steve during an interview, "Steve, you have thousands of employees, dozens of businesses and hotel casinos all over the world. How do you ensure that each guest has the same experience that we are talking about here today?" To which Steve replied with, "It's all about the company culture. If our staff believes they are being paid fairly and treated with respect, they will do the best that they can for our guests."

Let's make this clear right now. Money doesn't motivate people. People motivate people. It doesn't matter how much you pay somebody because if they're unhappy in their position (or more commonly, their life) they will not do a good job. Fire fast, hire slow. Don't ask anything of your employees that you wouldn't do yourself. At the end of the day the most important thing is that people feel appreciated. You can't always milk the cow, you have to feed it too.

Cite 15

**Armoured Vehicles Story**

Prior to getting into real estate, I worked for an automotive vehicle manufacturer building custom luxury SUVs for high net worth individuals. This place was really badass. We were making million-dollar trucks by hand with three inch thick glass and cappuccino machines. My tenure in the company was about three years in length and when I first took on the position it was a very fulfilling opportunity. The people in the shop were fantastic and welcoming, and the management was pretty good as well. About eighteen months in, "something" started to change, and it was predominantly from the management level. I realized at that time that the attitude from the top has a trickle-down effect to the attitudes of those that work on the shop floor. I remember succinctly having it out with the owner of the company (which looking back was probably rather presumptuous, but it taught me a valuable lesson).

Around that time, I noticed that the upper brass were not looking after their employees, and I had never owned a business at this time nor did I fully understand the gravity of what may have been taking place in the background. From this very low-level and looking up, I realized that if the management doesn't look after their staff, there wouldn't be anybody to manage. So, I mentioned this to the owner rather firmly and I said to him, "Sir, if you don't look after your people, who's going to be here to build your trucks?" He had no answer for me and said, "Ryan, don't worry about it, you just continue on with your day and I'll continue on with mine." I thought to myself, "Fuck you buddy, I may not know much about much, but I do know if that the shop floor is empty, we will all be out of a job together and that means you too…"

Sure enough, mass layoffs took place, and everybody was out of a job with the exception of a couple people who hung around for the next year or two during transition to company shut down. What really got me about this place was that the concept was amazing, and the people were so talented, but the direction of the company completely tanked. Would it have been so bad to come out and say "thanks" from time to time? Would it have been so bad to drop a compliment from time to time? Would it have been so catastrophic to the bottom line to send the guys home early on the Friday of a long weekend or show up with some pizza?

**Family Owner Labour Story**

Growing up I realized something very interesting about many of the male figures in my life—they were all self-employed. My dad, my uncles, a significant amount of my friends' parents are all self-employed and subliminally self-motivated. I specifically remember seeing one of my uncles, who co-owned a concrete block manufacturing facility, working in and on his business. The guy was a hard worker no question about it. I worked at the facility for a little bit doing welding and odd jobs, and during my brief tenure there, I observed something interesting.

Once or twice a week he would come out of the office and work the assembly line. Sometimes this was for a simple straightforward task, and other times it was physically laborious work. He would come out in his boots, grab a block, throw it in the tumbler, and move on to the next position. I realized quickly that people respected him for this. They didn't see him as just the boss in the office. They saw him as a guy who understood them and the work they did. I carry this mentality through to my business activity today. Try it for yourself: Chip in, help out, tell the staff how great they are doing, send a gift card to someone who's having a rough week, or grab some food from the local pub. It's a great feeling.

## 3.13 #THEHIGHESTANDBESTUSE OF FINANCING

*"Using a credit card for something like a house is unconventional…"*

**Bank Financing/A-Lenders**

**If you qualify for A-lender bank financing, you will receive the best and most** competitive rates available for buying real estate. In Canada, the most common investment property loan-to-value is 20% down payment, and in addition to this, there are government-backed insurers that will insure mortgages in the 5–19% LTV space. There are often no direct fees or legal costs associated with financing through A-lenders, and most variable mortgages can be broken with a three-month interest penalty.

*Insurance Premium*

A typical premium from these insurers is upwards of 4.5% and this premium is tacked onto your overall mortgage and will be paid out of the proceeding twenty-five to forty years of the amortized loan. Note, interest is charged on this insurance premium in the same way that more borrowed money would be. In the multi-family building space, CMHC will reduce your monthly payment by permitting an extended amortization up to thirty-five years on existing buildings, or forty years on new construction. It will also provide you with a lower annual interest rate, that over the duration of the term will recapture the expense of the upfront CMHC premium. Higher cash flow for some investors would be considered #TheHighestAndBestUse.

**Private money**

Private money is the most expensive money when comparing to other lending institutions, but also offers the most flexibility for purchasing smashed-up assets. In the case of many investors seeking off market deals, value-add plays, non-occupied buildings, or half renovated projects, private money is the only way that they can borrow funds to close a transaction.

Some lenders require collateral or a registration title, and some lenders will do this by way of promissory note. Whichever direction your lender and you decide to be suitable for the project, always put the relationship first. The borrower needs to understand that the investor is investing in them first and the property second. The investor needs to understand the importance of a borrower's track record and how that may affect the outcome of the deal.

Mortgage brokers that deal in private money will typically underwrite a deal based on loan-to-value and place lesser emphasis on the back story of the borrower. As a borrower myself, I prefer to work directly with lenders where possible so that a long-term relationship can be established.

**Vacant Land/Construction Financing**

Vacant land financing is considered a specialty market and often pushed into the private money space. Most institutional lenders do not finance vacant land as it is seen as risky, and the bank does not want to own your asset. They are not in the real estate business, they are in the lending business.

Construction financing ties in with vacant land closely as the most common use for vacant land is to build something upon it. Many lenders will consider a set percentage of the construction cost plus land value in their underwriting to determine how much money is to be leant on the deal. Construction financing can be cumbersome at times, so you need to weigh the pros and cons to see if the underwriting process is worth the wait.

**B-Lender**

The B-lender space is sometimes considered "shadow lending" because they underwrite their deals differently than an A-lender bank does. A B-lender often charges fees and a higher interest for a loan in exchange for added flexibility on debt service or income qualification method. If a borrower doesn't qualify at the A-lender bank level, they may still have an opportunity to qualify in the B-lender space. Although paying fees and extra interest comes at a financial cost, #TheHighestAndBestUse of B-lenders may save you in overall cost if it means you can continue to grow your portfolio as the sole owner on a property.

**Vendor Take Back**

The vendor take back (VTB) has been instrumental in so many creative financing deals for me and countless investors that buy real estate. A VTB in simple terms is also known as "seller financing" and is such that the seller carries a mortgage for the buyer in the same manner that a bank would lend the buyer money.

In Canada, some benefits to the seller would be a tax deferral for up to five years on the gain from the disposition and residual income every month after the property has sold. A VTB can be secured in first, second, or third plus position depending on the circumstance and typically involves no qualification process. The seller at this point would be hands-off on the property, and the buyer would carry on their ownership tenure from closing day forward.

## Credit Cards/Lines of Credit

Credit cards and lines of credit are another great way to finance purchases, construction, or similar cash call requirements when short-term funding is needed.

Credit cards come with cash advance or point-of-sale opportunities to borrow money at interest rates set out by the lender. Credit cards are often high interest rate (20% or more) so they need to be utilized with care. Some highest and best use techniques on credit cards would be balance transfers (send money to another credit card for a small fee), collecting points, paying one card with the next, using perks that the credit card company offers to achieve discounts at local retailers, or using the cash advance feature. Provided the card is paid off before the monthly term is up, the buyers typically pay 0% interest.

Hardware store cards also fit into this category and often give you point-of-sale discounts or other perks in store that non-contract accounts wouldn't get. #TheHighestAndBestUse use tip on these would be to use a hardware store card for the full duration of interest free availability (let's say forty days), and then pay that card with another credit card (additional forty days). If the billing dates align correctly, you will buy yourself eighty days of interest free money. It is also quite common for hardware store credit cards to offer no payments for six to eighteen months. Take advantage of these if you feel your financial savvy is capable.

Lines of credit are similar to credit cards but can be turned into cash at much lower interest rates. An LOC can be secured against a property like a mortgage or can be unsecured and backed by the borrowers personal guarantee. Corporations and individuals can get lines of credit.

*Chapter 3.00 : #TheHighestAndBestUse of "Your Skill Sets and Time"*

> **Buying a House With a Credit Card - #TheHighestAndBestUse Story**
>
> *During an off-market mailer campaign, a lead came in from a lady and her husband looking to sell their home. They didn't want any fuss, or any showings, and wanted to sell the house privately. I went over to the property and quickly noted that they, in fact, were interested in moving forward with a transaction such as this and that the property needed considerable repairs. After we negotiated the particulars, the deal was sent off to the lawyers and the closing date quickly approached.*
>
> *During this time, I had several projects underway and I had always wanted to close on a house using a credit card. Using a credit card for something like a house is unconventional, and typically not done, so I figured it was worth a shot. I called my lawyer's office and asked if this was possible, and they said that it was, but they would have to charge me a 2.5% fee to cover the transactional costs. In true #TheHighestAndBestUse fashion and to avoid the 2.5% fee (but still close with my credit card), I did a cash advance over multiple cards for the full price of the home. This cash was converted to a bank draft, and the bank draft satisfied the closing requirements.*
>
> *The property closed as scheduled, and with $0 of my own money.*

## 3.14 Maximizing Your Daily Efficiency

> *"Unless your conversation has purpose, there is time for leisure somewhere else, you have stuff to do."*

There are several different ways to arrange your day for maximum efficiency depending on lifestyle and how involved with the business you are. For me, the following is what works:

### *Mornings*

My mornings are broken up into fifteen-minute time blocks. Typically speaking, anything from 6:00 a.m. until noon is considered "existing business." I've chosen to do it this way because a team needs to start their day with quality direction. Suppliers call, contractors have questions, people need advice, coaching clients find deals from the night before, lots of stuff happens. Some of these tasks may be delegated to others such as a site supervisor or manager and some of these tasks might be better handled by you directly. How your business is structured is up to you, just know that people need the most assistance before noon.

### *Noon*

From 12:00 pm to 1:00 pm, I try where possible to consider this personal time. Some executives like to power nap, some prefer yoga, some eat lunch or have a stretch, possibly even go for a walk with your phone turned off. Personal time is very important. I didn't realize this until later on in my career after I noticed that sometimes you need to slow down in order the speed up.

An interesting point about napping: A thirty-minute nap may appear to yield thirty minutes less in available productivity, however, I have personally felt that daily naps reduce stress levels and extend your productive working capacity by sixty net minutes. That's a 200% return on time. Try going for a nap with a small problem in mind. When you wake up, focus and clarity will realign and the solution may appear.

### *Afternoon*

From 1:00 p.m. until 6:00 p.m., this is considered new business time blocking. Perhaps you're reaching out for new business, or going to see properties, or locking down a supplier deal that will save you 4% on materials. Whatever this looks like for you, new business should be considered in the afternoon. This is also a fantastic time to return phone calls or craft up new emails left behind from the day before. Many business owners time block a specific time to return calls and they put that in their voicemail message. For example, "Thank you for calling, please leave a voicemail, and also note that I return calls between 2:00 p.m. and 3:00 pm. Thank you."

A quick note about time blocking in the afternoon, if you're operating on fifteen-minute time blocks like I do, make sure you stick to those. Leave buffer zones between tasks in order to maximize efficiency of your day and if in the event something spills over you don't impact the next task, phone call, or meeting.

Consider time for things like physical travel time if going from one location to the next. Having a bit of slush between tasks is also a good time to recharge your batteries, if need be, depending on the daily challenges. It is so easy to get sucked into casual nonproductive conversation or small talk about your cat. Nobody cares about your cat like you do, so move on. Unless your conversation has purpose, there is time for leisure somewhere else, you have stuff to do.

### *Evening*

Evening time is yours to choose—some people like to work in the evening because they are most creative at this hour. Some like it for family because that's when the kids are home from school or their spouse is off work. If you're a nighthawk, late evening productivity after everyone in your household is in bed, might also be the best time for you to reflect on your day or make adjustments to your schedule.

### *Early Morning or Pre-Bedtime*

This is an ideal time for mind feeding. Listen to an audio book, read a physical book, watch a documentary, or take an online course. Put the day in front/behind you and focus on where you're heading next with new skills or strategy. Very important. Don't skimp here. This is 100% #TheHighestAndBestUse of your time.

## 3.15 Eliminating Time Suckers

*"Movement is inefficient."*

**Brace for impact here:** This might upset some folks, and also happens to be one of my favourite topics. Things like social media, email, telephone, casual strolls in the park, and other distractions, whatever it is that isn't purposeful and a direct reason why your business is succeeding, needs to be removed from your day.

### *Social Media*

YouTube, Twitter, Instagram, Snapchat, Facebook, etc. Cut this shit out right now. Turn off all of your notifications immediately. Every time a buzzer goes off on your phone, there is this natural inclination to check out what that really meant. Who's interested in my picture? Who wants to invite me to the next party? Who commented on my short video clip? Who cares. Save a set amount of time per day to go through and rattle off some responses to those that matter most and get back to work. Make your posts and uploads at this time as well so people online know you're a real business.

Science: There is a dopamine-hit science behind the way that social media actually functions, and every time somebody is interested in what you have to say or something that you posted for others to view, it gives you an internal high. It's with this internal high that comes the feeling of being wanted. Everybody wants to be wanted but not everybody can have a successful business. Nine out of ten entrepreneurs fail in the first five years. Don't be one of those people who got caught in the trap of distraction.

Cite 16

### *Emails*

Unless your job is specifically to respond to emails/something similar, time block a set period to get these done in an orderly fashion. Do what works best for you. If it's once per hour, great; if it's once per day, great. Everybody has a different business and different workflow. Turn off notifications if not absolutely necessary/your prime form of communication to the outside world, as this will distract you from your tasks.

### *Telephone*

If you are the one that handles phone calls directly in your business, be aware how much time this can take and the mental gear changing that may be required to get back into your stream of focus after this activity. If you have an answering service or an assistant that can handle some of this workload for you, it will help you be more productive. If the calls are urgent in nature, take them right away, especially if it's something that will propel your day forward and improve the efficiency of others. Incoming calls such as the bank, government, or a call centre that would take hours to get back in touch with could be considered priority because getting those people on the line is a task in itself. Weigh the pros and cons.

## *Physical Mail*

If you have the opportunity for someone to assist you in opening your mail, it will save you time. I hate opening my own mail. Yes, I still get physical mail, that is the nature of my business and it's something that is unavoidable. This is a task that is easily delegated to somebody close to you that you trust, and just know that the person opening your mail will read it. People are curious.

## *Traveling*

Physical travel is one of the biggest time suckers you can possibly do. Write this down, "movement is inefficient." Write it down again. When I say movement is inefficient, I really truly mean it. The construction business can soak up your entire day by being on the road and travelling from site to site as a business owner. Get good at communicating by telephone, email, or text with your clients, your team, and service providers. It's amazing what can take place in five minutes with the telephone call and a quick picture message versus actually going somewhere to see the problem. Video calls are the new normal, and they are very inexpensive.

Benchmark the cost of your fuel, mileage, wear and tear, time away from something else of importance. Sometimes it may feel frustrating or unproductive to do it in this manner, however, 99% of the time it is the best way to go. Are some things unavoidable? Yes. If required, go see it in the flesh. But for the most part, work on these skills, hone them, and take your time back. In addition, hire someone on your staff to do these onsite tasks where you deem appropriate, this might be #TheHighestAndBestUse of their time.

One more note on travelling, in particular by road vehicle. Consider the cost benefits of hiring a driving service to take you where you want to go. There is a pro/con associated with owning a vehicle, having insurance, maintaining that vehicle, filling it with fuel, and driving it yourself. Depending on your hourly value as a business owner, it might make sense to have a driving service cruise you around town so you can be productive in the back seat. This doesn't have to be a person named Watson wearing a top hat and opening up your Bentley. This can be as simple as an Uber/Lyft driver picking you up and taking you to your cottage. The point is, while you're driving, you're not fully focusing on a business-related task. The economics here are simple: if you could be negotiating a flip from the comfort of an Uber X vs. driving yourself through downtown streets to seek a parking space, you've left money on the table.

Like many, if you consider driving yourself to be your preferred method of transportation, schedule your phone calls on a Bluetooth hands-free device in advance to make the best use of your seat-time. A short list from your daily agenda will suffice and help keep your eyes on the road, while still making progress. Podcasts and audio books are also an excellent way to convert being stuck in traffic into a productive educational experience.

**Food**

*Groceries*

If you are used to cooking your own meals and buying your own groceries, it's time to change. When you go for groceries, it's four hours out of your day whether you know it or not. You make the list, contemplate the list, get in the car, drive to the store, shop around for an hour or two, bag it, bring it home, unload it into the house, pack it away in the fridge, and now your energy is somewhere else. Mentally you are in a disadvantaged position because you're thinking about that bag of oranges that rolled over in your front seat.

This is a major time sucker that can be delegated. Get a grocery delivery service (at a bare minimum) that shops for you and drops it in your trunk. Pay by credit card through an app or better yet, have deliveries brought right to your front door. There are tons of services that deliver organic fruit and vegetables in addition to pre-prepared foods, this includes the small chains and bigger retail outlets.

*Personal Chef vs. Takeout*

Hire a personal chef or order takeout. The amount of time spent preparing your meals is absolutely ridiculous. Have you ever cut vegetables for a stir fry? Insanity. This activity could be costing you more (dollars) than you think provided your time spent working on something business related is of higher value.

Ordering takeout on apps like Skip the Dishes, Uber Eats, Don't Cook Just Eat, etc. is brilliant. Does it "cost" more upfront to order something and have it dropped off? Yeah, for sure. But it's how we define "cost" that is the true difference.

We will discuss this in a case study below.

## Food Case Studies:

*Case Study 1 - Entertainment/Emotional Perspective*

Let's say you finish up work at 5:00 p.m. and are the primary meal maker for your household. You think about dinner all day long (the dreaded "what am I going to make tonight"), gather the food, prepare the meal, dirty the dishes, plate the food, wash the dishes, and finally crash to bed. There's two hours gone, excluding the time it took for you to shop and get the food to begin with.

Consider ordering takeout or using meal services locally such as small-town restaurants or the apps mentioned above. There are probably a dozen services out there that will bring food to your doorstep without having to do all of the preparation. Spend the would-be prep time working on your business to cover the cost of having somebody else prepare your meal and you will double win. Not only will you get further ahead with that "procrastinated thing" you're working on, but you will also be able to eat some tremendous food from different restaurants that you wouldn't have otherwise had the opportunity to experience.

Let's just assume that the cost for eating this way is above the cost of you preparing your own food. Isn't it kind of fun to try different meals anyways? There is an entertainment/emotional factor involved in this capacity. Consider the cost of utilities in your calculations as well.

*Case Study 2 - Financial Perspective*

Details: Your billable time is $30/hour. You can make a meal for two people at $16 worth of food cost/utilities. In comparison, the cost for those meals via takeout is $42 after delivery.

What we must do is separate the base food cost if you cook DIY ($16) from the up charge in restaurant labour to have that meal in ready to eat/delivered format ($42 ready to eat/delivered). Thus, $42 delivered - $16 DIY = $26 in additional spending. The figure to benchmark your time against is $26.

In this case, let's assume the DIY meal would take you a simple one hour to prepare and fully clean up. If you ordered the $42 delivered meal, and spent that one hour of would-be cooking and clean up time actually working on your business at the $30/hour rate, then you would be financially ahead by $4. Multiply this out x three meals per day, 365 days per year. That's $4,380 in your pocket plus forward movement on your business, and you have a full-time cloud kitchen at your disposal. The specifics of food cost, food quality, and preference will vary depending on how you eat. Just know that this maneuver is #TheHighestAndBestUse of your time, and if you're focusing on a couple dollars here or there, it's distracting you from the bigger picture.

Think about this, if your hourly rate was higher, or lower, how would that affect this model? How would your mental state be if you took this one chore off of your to-do list and it wasn't for monetary gain? How much time do you spend shopping for the food and putting it away? What about food waste? Consider asking yourself these questions.

*Cooking for Efficiency*
If you must make a meal or need to feed a small army of children, do so in bulk. Lasagnas, casseroles, soups, pasta with sauce, assorted meat, full turkey, etc. If the grill is on, it takes the same effort to cook one burger as it does ten. Leftovers are delicious anyhow. Freezer meals that are ready to go in the oven can also be a lifesaver.

**Maintenance Services Around the Home**
Big "time sucker" maintenance tasks around your home would include things like lawn care, snow removal, laundry, or odd handyman chores that can be done by somebody else. Using the example above making $30 per hour, if you can hire the neighbour at $14 per hour to cut your grass, for every hour that you are both working you will net a positive $16 in your favour. The same thing goes for snow removal—shoveling your own driveway for the purposes of just getting it done is a waste of your time and can be done by somebody else.

As a sidebar to this, there are two caveats that need to be discussed:

1. Exercise
2. Work Ethic

Currently, I cut my own grass. This is not financial reasoning, this is so that I actually get out of my seat and move. You can delegate your life away such that you do nothing, pay for everything, and turn into a slob. I cut the grass by choice, not by necessity.

Something else to note for those with children would be work ethic. If you want your children to grow up knowing that Mom and Dad have a good work ethic, consider cutting your own grass and plowing your own snow. Include them. This will instill quality values early on, and they will reap future mindset benefits that are predominantly nonfinancial.

Cleaning your house and laundry services would fall into the same category as cutting the grass and plowing the snow. If you can find somebody that you trust and that does a great job for you, then hire them so that you can focus on what you're actually good at doing. The fact is, most people can clean a house with some general effort and know-how but not everybody can operate a business successfully. You, as a business operator, need to focus on what you're good at doing and stop splitting that focus on other household chores. There are some fantastic service providers out there that can help you with this.

**Business Related**

*Meetings*
Inefficient meetings are ultimate time suckers. If you don't need to meet in person, do not. This stems back to movement being inefficient and how you value your time. Remember, your time is precious and you can't get it back. I get bummed if I lose money, but I get pissed if someone takes my time. If you work in an office environment, walk and talk. If you work from home, do a video conference with a time limit. Always have a time limit and always have somewhere else to be (because it's typically true) or you will end up in small talk about the weather. Be cordial, be succinct and to the point, and don't forget to have some fun, but get the job done and move on. Read a book called *The Gold Standard* by Ari Gold, a character from the HBO TV show *Entourage*. He's brilliant in this regard.

*Lunches and Coffees*
These can be a large time commitment. By the time you leave your place of business, drive to where you need to be, park, eat, chat, depart, and get back to your desk you've killed at least two to three hours depending on traffic. This is counterproductive the majority of the time if you aren't laser focused on the reason for doing so.

Are there times that a lunch is important or needed? Yes, 100%. These should be accepted with grace and enjoyed. There is no replacement for an in-person connection should the situation arise. Be selective. Also know that if you're asking someone to lunch, perhaps there is a more effective way that you can get their feedback or do a deal without physically getting together. Their time is valuable too.

*The News*
Watching the news will eat you up and spit you out. These shows are the absolute definition of pessimism and are the absolute bottom of the barrel. The media has a unique way of creating fear in any situation to grab headlines and keep you living in mediocrity. Enough of that. Elections, shootings, murders, disease, famine, fire/floods, theft, and unemployment. Awful stuff. Acknowledge that these things are out there in the world, and you may feel fortunate to live where you do. First world countries have it unbelievably good. Now turn the fucking news off and focus on winning. There will always be a reason to do, or not to do, something.

*Bottom Line*
Define #TheHighestAndBestUse of your time because time is the ultimate commodity.

## 3.16 Passive vs. Active Investing

*"Money talks, wealth whispers."*

**A large component to growing your business is defining if you're an active of** passive investor. Below we will discuss what each stream involves, and what #TheHighestAndBestUse of these options may be for you.

*Active Investor:*
Commonly referred to as the working/active partner, this person is the do'er in the case of real estate transactions. They are finding the property, coordinating the contractors, running the numbers, and popping in tenants. The active partner is boots-on-the-ground resources for the passive partner, and the active partner is giving up time (sweat equity) in exchange for the opportunity to be financed by a passive investor.

Active streams of investment here may be flipping, wholesaling, buy/fix/refinance and hold rentals, rent to own, multifamily apartment buildings, or land development/new construction.

*Passive Investor*

The passive partner in real estate investing is most often the brains and/or the money to the operation. The passive partner has often already built their wealth and is looking to have their money work for them. Streams of investment here are commonly first/second/third mortgages, promissory notes, construction financing, down payment and bank financing qualification, or similar. Passive opportunities may also involve the active streams mentioned above, with someone else (active partner) doing the work, which in turn provides the passive opportunity being sought. In general terms, return on time is very high in the passive investment space, with a lower ROI than the active investment space.

A passive partner needs to focus on security of their capital, the return generated, and the speed at which it takes place. These are the steps to follow, in order.

1. *Security* - This is done in two ways: The first way is investing in conservatively leveraged properties where if the active investor defaults, the passive investor can safely reclaim their money. The second way, and most importantly, is the security generated from a trusted active investor with a track record. Remember, a good investor can turn around a bad deal, and a bad investor will destroy a good deal. Invest in the person first, it's not about the property.

2. *Returns* - What is the ROI on the investment? How much money does the passive investor put in the deal vs. getting back upon completion? Are there any other advantages like brand awareness, market share, media attention, or industry connections that may come alongside with the investment? These are intangibles that don't correlate directly to "making money now" and may provide future benefits in addition to income generation over and above the base fundamentals.

3. *Speed* - How long will it take to achieve the expected return? Does a 6% return happen over three months? Or three years?

## 3.17 Educating Yourself

*"With free content, you get generic advice that could or could not apply to you."*

### *Books*

**"There is no difference between a person who does not read, and a person who** cannot read" ~ Mark Twain

The world's top CEOs read a minimum of one book per month, all the way up to one book per week. This is a proven fact. Since, as discussed earlier, CEOs rule by strategy not by tactic, any 1% advantage that you can have over the competition with something that you picked up from (yep, you guessed it) a book will yield tremendous results when amortized over the years or spread over multiple operations. There is no better way to educate yourself on a dollars-spent basis than reading a book. This is the most inexpensive and direct way to drill down on any topic that you could ever think of. Want to learn how to paint? Get a book. Want to learn how to sew? Get a book. Want to learn how to grow tomato plants? Get a book. Want to learn how to completely crush it in real estate? ...

Books are something that people never throw away.

### *Audio books:*

Audio books are another fantastic way to make use of downtime sitting in traffic or driving somewhere (as previously mentioned), and also the preferred method of learning for auditory learners. In the last number of years, an increasing amount of authors have converted paper copy to digital audio books that can be downloaded from services like Amazon's Audible or streamed on YouTube. A great way to get audio books for free is to register with your local public library. Most people don't know this, but libraries rent audio books by the week and they generally come at no cost provided if you are a resident of that particular city. Sign up online or go into the physical library location, register for a library card, and you're good to go.

Sometimes you will find audio books there that can't be found from conventional online services so there is some benefit to doing this. If you're on a budget and just starting out, this is absolutely the best thing you can do. Save yourself the

$20–30 a month on a subscription somewhere and just grab the audio books for free. If you're travelling long distance or via airplane, physical books get cumbersome.

### *Online Education*

Online education is one of the biggest industries of this generation. Every paid ad on social media says, "Buy this over here, buy that over there," and they're not totally wrong but they're not totally right either. There's a lot of quality content out there that will truly benefit your life and there's also a lot of garbage that's hollow and strictly intended to separate you from your dollars. Sift through and do what's best for your business/lifestyle. In the end, any content or training requires decisive action to make it work.

I'm a believer that YouTube has benefited my life because prior to getting into real estate, I didn't know the cost of a 2x4. I've guest spoken about this exact thing on several podcasts and when I say I didn't know, I really (really) didn't know what building materials to buy, how to renovate, the cost of things, how real estate transactions work—I knew nothing. You can go on YouTube or Google and search for free content on whatever topic it is that you're looking for, and there's a pretty good chance that you will find a base level of help. Always exhaust all of your free options before hiring paid advice.

With free content, you get generic advice that could or could not apply to you. Sales training is a prime example about one person's selling style over another. Clothing, same thing. What one person says looks great (a three-piece suit) might be stodgy and stuck up to the next stylist who is recommending yoga pants and a Tilley hat. Take heed of personal preference and personal style, and pick a system that works best for you that doesn't conflict with all of the other things that you're trying to achieve

### *Get a Coach*

If you're going out in the market and spending lots of money on growing your business, for God's sake, just get a coach. Education is like a stove, buy it once and use it forever. It doesn't go bad, it doesn't expire, and what you learn today will be tweaked and modified for the next wave of trends ten years down the road. In the same manner that electronic music is a revision of disco from the 1970s, hip hop has also evolved and rock n' roll will never die. Everything is the same, just recycled and renewed with a special flair and a special twist based on the times.

The Beatles learned from Chuck Berry, Tony Robbins learned from Jim Rohn, and Wayne Gretzky learned from Walter Gretzky. The best performers have coaches because they see things in you that you can't see in yourself. Tailored advice is the key.

#TheHighestAndBestUse *Brief Story*
"When You Want to Succeed as Bad as You Want to Breathe, Then You'll Be Successful."

In the mid-2000s, a public speaker by the name of Eric Thomas succeeded with a hit viral video on YouTube. This video, in effect, was him telling his mentor that he wanted to be successful.

His mentor asked Eric "how bad" he wanted to be successful, to which Eric replied with "really bad." So his mentor said, "Ok, fine, I'll meet you at 2:00 a.m. tomorrow morning at the lake." So Eric meets his mentor at the lake and after a series of conversations his mentor walks out in the water, turns to Eric, and says, "Walk with me." Eric steps out. The mentor steps out just a little further. Eric steps out just a little further.

His mentor says, "Ok, just come a little more," and Eric begrudgingly says, "Hey, why are we doing this?" In a split second, his mentor grabs Eric's head and submerges it below the surface. As Eric is wiggling and squirming and splashing around, his mentor lets him back up. As he's gasping for air, his mentor once again dunks Eric's head under the surface. Seconds later, he pulls Eric up for good. Gathering his composure, Eric says to his mentor, "What was that for?" His mentor says, "When You Want to Succeed as Bad as You Want to Breathe, Then You'll Be Successful."

In this situation there was no way for Eric's mentor to fully explain to him the importance of dedication and focus in the same manner as that which had taken place—it's something that had to be felt.

> *Action item: Try it from your seat. Stop reading the book, (and without harming yourself) hold your breath for a bit. At some point when your body says it needs air, you'll understand.*

# #TheHighestAndBestUse
## Golden Nuggets of "Your Own Skill Sets and Time"

## The Ten Mile Rule/Go West chapter -- Ref #1

### Reference Cites:

https://www.familysearch.org/wiki/en/Ontario_Additional_Land_Records_(National_Institute)

https://www.toronto.com/opinion-story/6217138-the-amateur-genealogist-land-records-surveying/

Digital historical land maps in Ontario can be found here: https://www.arcgis.com/apps/webappviewer/index.html?id=8cc6be34f6b54992b27da17467492d2f

https://www.thecanadianencyclopedia.ca/en/article/township

https://www.thecanadianencyclopedia.ca/en/article/territorial-evolution

https://www.youtube.com/watch?v=3PWWtqfwacQ&ab_channel=WendoverProductions

https://www.youtube.com/watch?v=3MlyAvUfh8E&ab_channel=Cheddar

## Land Ownership History -- Ref #2

### References:

https://en.wikipedia.org/wiki/History_of_Canada

https://en.wikipedia.org/wiki/The_Canadian_Crown_and_Indigenous_peoples_of_Canada

https://en.wikipedia.org/wiki/Seigneurial_system_of_New_France

https://en.wikipedia.org/wiki/Allodial_title

https://olta.ca/wp-content/uploads/2013/03/Part-1-Real-Estate-Basics.pdf

https://www.thecanadianencyclopedia.ca/en/article/concession-line

https://www.thecanadianencyclopedia.ca/en/article/territorial-evolution

https://www.adventurecanada.com/atlantic-canada-sable-island-and-gulf-of-saint-lawrence/a-brief-history-of-saint-pierre-and-miquelon

https://en.wikipedia.org/wiki/History_of_Saint_Pierre_and_Miquelon#:~:text=By%20the%20end%20of%20the,%22abri%22%20for%20the%20fishermen.

### Cite #3

**Research Cites:**

http://www.ontarioprospectors.com/news/0708SurfaceOwnerBrochure.pdf

https://www.capp.ca/explore/mineral-rights/

https://www.canaryinstitute.ca/publications/Understanding_Mining_Rts.pdf

https://www.lexology.com/library/detail.aspx?g=d73e5631-70d9-4d27-a24e-89a50b123877

### Cite #4

**Cites:**

https://en.wikipedia.org/wiki/Crown_land

https://www.thecanadianencyclopedia.ca/en/article/crown-land#:~:text=Crown%20land%20is%20the%20term,the%20federal%20or%20provincial%20governments.&text=Less%20than%2011%25%20of%20Canada's,the%20federal%20or%20provincial%20governments.

https://www.ontario.ca/page/recreational-activities-on-crown-land

### Cite 5

https://www.ontario.ca/page/ownership-determination-beds-navigable-waters-act-policy)

### Cite 6

**Cites:**

https://www.hauseit.com/air-rights-nyc/#:~:text=Air%20rights%20are%20sold%20and,floors%20of%20the%20developer's%20building.

https://en.wikipedia.org/wiki/Air_rights

https://webdocs.edmonton.ca/zoningbylaw/ZoningBylaw/Part1/Interpretive/6_1_Definitions/Floor_Area_Ratio.htm

https://www.nytimes.com/2018/03/02/nyregion/jp-morgan-chase-midtown-east-air-rights.html

https://www.toronto.com/news-story/9810277-toronto-mayor-backs-push-to-expropriate-air-rights-for-rail-deck-park/

**Cite 6.5**

https://en.wikipedia.org/wiki/Seigneurial_system_of_New_France

**Cite 7**

**Cites:**

Oshawa ZBL 60-94   www.oshawa.ca

https://en.wikipedia.org/wiki/Easement#:~:text=The%20party%20gaining%20the%20benefit,gain%20access%20to%20A's%20house.

https://www.hummingbirdlaw.com/squatters-rights/

**Cite 7.5**

Telephone coaching session with Stefan Aarnio, year 2018.

**Cite 8**

See page 15 of http://www.mah.gov.on.ca/AssetFactory.aspx?did=10267 and add it into the book.

**Cite 8.5**

https://www.ontario.ca/page/ownership-determination-beds-navigable-waters-act-policy

**Cite 9**

Cites for all land division related:

https://www.vaughan.ca/services/business/part_lot_control_bylaws/Pages/default.aspx

https://www.woodbull.ca/practice-areas/details/planning-and-development/consents-(severances)-part-lot-control-exemptions

http://www.mah.gov.on.ca/AssetFactory.aspx?did=10267   (Large PDF about consent from Ontario government, some good diagrams, page seven and beyond, good handouts as well and check lists, could take a lot of info from here for online course, tons of checklists.)

https://environmentaldefence.ca/2020/08/28/may-never-heard-ministers-zoning-order-used-ok-not-anymore/

https://www.protectyourboundaries.ca/downloads/ProtectYourBoundaries-Legal%20Descriptions.pdf (great Pdf on understanding legal description,)

https://www.ontario.ca/document/citizens-guide-land-use-planning/local-planning-appeal-tribunal#section-2

## Cite 9.5

Point Roberts documentary: https://www.youtube.com/watch?v=ARYL03Dq8cg

## Cite 10

**Cites:**

Multiple lot types: https://journal.firsttuesday.us/type-of-lots/70394/

https://www.gimme-shelter.com/lot-shape-50068/

## Cite 11

**Cites:**

https://crtc.gc.ca/eng/archive/1999/DT99-13.htm

## Cite 11.5

https://en.wikipedia.org/wiki/Cloud_seeding#:~:text=Cloud%20seeding%20is%20a%20type,microphysical%20processes%20within%20the%20cloud.

## Cite 12

**Add article to website:**

https://lasvegassun.com/news/2000/apr/28/wynn-buys-di/

https://www.reviewjournal.com/business/tourism/wynn-to-host-last-round-of-golf-before-paradise-park-construction/

https://www.cnbc.com/2016/05/25/wynns-answer-to-nevada-drought-a-massive-waterpark.html

## Cite 13

**Cites:**

https://en.wikipedia.org/wiki/One_Times_Square

https://en.wikipedia.org/wiki/Times_Square

## Cite 14

https://en.wikipedia.org/wiki/33_Thomas_Street

https://www.investopedia.com/articles/active-trading/042414/youd-better-know-your-highfrequency-trading-terminology.asp

## Cite 15

https://www.youtube.com/watch?v=m9Lg7uKhTMs&t=3s

https://www.youtube.com/watch?v=eOesXyfJGI0

https://www.youtube.com/watch?v=GeuAvVBqUvU

## Cite 16

https://sitn.hms.harvard.edu/flash/2018/dopamine-smartphones-battle-time/

## Cite 17

https://www.forbes.com/sites/neilpatel/2015/01/16/90-of-startups-will-fail-heres-what-you-need-to-know-about-the-10/?sh=503f179a6679

# CLOSING REMARKS

Thank you for reading The Highest And Best Use Playbook: Finding the Unfair Advantage Over Your Real Estate Competition.

Follow Along With Us and Stay Connected

Website: TheHighestAndBestUse.com
Podcast: The Highest and Best Use Real Estate Podcast with Ryan Carr
Coaching Info: TheHighestAndBestUse.com
Facebook: https://www.facebook.com/thehighest.andbestuse
Instagram: @TheHighestAndBestUse
YouTube: The Highest And Best Use
#TheHighestAndBestUse

**Other Contacts:**

Website: rwcarrinvestment.com
Facebook: R.W. Carr Investment Co
Instagram: @rwcarrinvestmentco
YouTube links: RW Carr Investment Co

## About the Author:

Ryan Carr is a Canadian real estate entrepreneur from the Greater Toronto Area. He specializes in finding the highest and best use of real property and coaching others to do the same.

Starting his real estate journey in 2012 with a bank-sale purchase, he has since grown his net worth and rental portfolio to become a self-made multimillionaire before age thirty. Ryan is an investor, a public speaker, a coach, and a podcast host.

Follow along at
www.TheHighestAndBestUse.com

www.ingramcontent.com/pod-product-compliance
Lightning Source LLC
Chambersburg PA
CBHW051330110526
44590CB00032B/4471